Editors
Mary S. Jones, M.A.
Erica N. Russikoff, M.A.

Editor in Chief
Karen J. Goldfluss, M.S. Ed.

Cover Artist
Tony Carrillo

Art Coordinator
Renée Mc Elwee

Illustrator
Clint McKnight

Imaging
James Edward Grace
Leonard P. Swierski

Publisher
Mary D. Smith, M.S. Ed.

Author
Ruth Foster, M. Ed.

Teacher Created Resources
6421 Industry Way
Westminster, CA 92683
www.teachercreated.com
ISBN: 978-1-4206-3977-3

Table of Contents

Introduction

The written word is a valuable and mighty tool. It allows us to communicate ideas, thoughts, feelings, and information. As with any tool, skill comes with practice. *Daily Warm-Ups: Nonfiction and Fiction Writing* uses high-interest and grade-level appropriate exercises to help develop confident, skilled writers.

This book is divided into seven sections. Each of the first six sections focuses on one of the following key writing traits. These traits have been identified by teachers as effective tools for improving student writing. The last section in the book offers a set of writing prompts to encourage further writing opportunities throughout the year.

Nonfiction and Fiction—Writing Traits Focus

IDEAS and CONTENT	VOICE
WORD CHOICE	ORGANIZATION
FLUENCY	CONVENTIONS

Daily Warm-Ups: Nonfiction and Fiction Writing uses a format that allows for flexibility in both instruction and learning. You may wish to begin with Warm-Up 1 and progress sequentially through all or most of the writing practices provided in the book. As an alternative, begin by introducing and modeling a specific writing trait that needs to be addressed. Students can then use the warm-ups within that section to practice and apply the trait as they complete each of the writing activities. Once the section is completed, continue working through the remaining sections based on the needs of the class.

With 150 independent warm-ups, there are plenty of writing opportunities to last the entire school year. As with any subject to be learned and mastered, writing should be continually practiced. With an arsenal of good writing techniques and an understanding of the writing process at their disposal, students can achieve a comfort level regardless of the writing task. Daily writing and guided practice using essential writing traits can help students reach a measurable level of success.

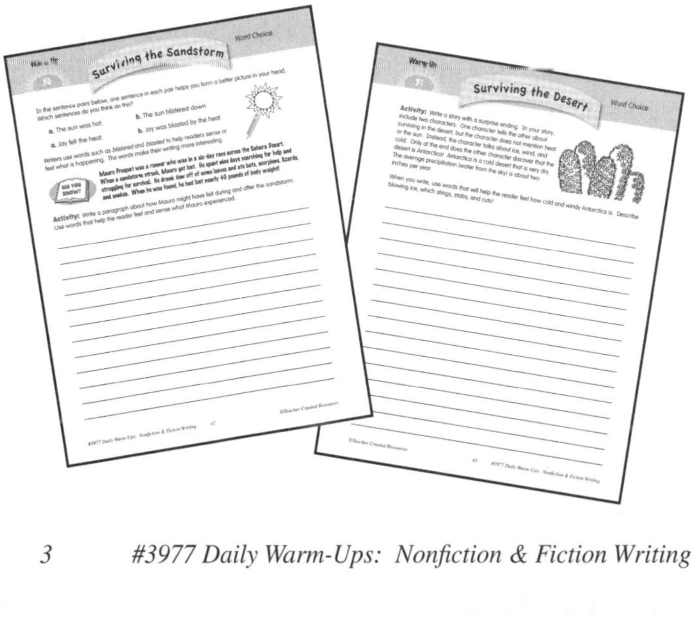

About This Book

The activities in this book were designed to help students gain experience writing in response to both nonfiction and fiction prompts. Each topic or theme includes pages that address both fiction and nonfiction writing.

The warm-up activities allow students to use both nonfiction and fiction writing on the same topic!

Warm-Up
46
It's About Time
Word Choice

It is two o'clock. Is it two in the morning or two in the afternoon? If it is 2:00 a.m., it is very early in the morning. If it is 2:00 p.m., it is in the afternoon.

When writers write about time, they often use other words or phrases besides *a.m.* and *p.m.* to let the reader know about the time. Words and phrases such as *sunrise, sunset, noon, midnight, at dawn, in the morning* and *in the evening* give the reader a sense of time without reading *a.m.* and *p.m.* over and over.

Activity: Describe a typical school day. Detail your morning routine and what you do at school, after school, and at night. Record all that you do at different times without writing *a.m.* and *p.m.* Instead, choose other words that will give your reader a sense of time.

Warm-Up
47
Time Mix-up
Word Choice

Activity: Write about a time when something went wrong. Perhaps someone missed an appointment, a train ride, or a plane flight. Or maybe someone went to see a movie at the wrong hour. Why did things go wrong? People had the wrong time! They mixed up *a.m.* and *p.m.* Remember to give your story a title.

Title:

These pages are about time. The first warm-up presents nonfiction information and asks the writer to prepare a response using the facts and ideas provided.

The second warm-up introduces the same topic in the form of a scenario and requires the student to write a response in the form of a fictional account.

The writing exercises in this book give students the opportunity to use a variety of writing formats. This allows a student to practice a specific writing skill while developing an understanding that good writing traits can be incorporated into a number of genres. The variation also keeps the daily writing activities exciting.

Each of the first six sections contains 25 warm-up writing pages that focus on the specific trait featured in the section.

The activities are written so that all students in a class can participate. While highly competent students may write more complex responses, all students will be able to practice writing at their respective levels of competence on a daily basis.

Each section ends with a page that incorporates both nonfiction and fiction writing activities. This page can be used as a culminating activity for the section, or as an informal assessment representative of the student's writing using the specific writing trait.

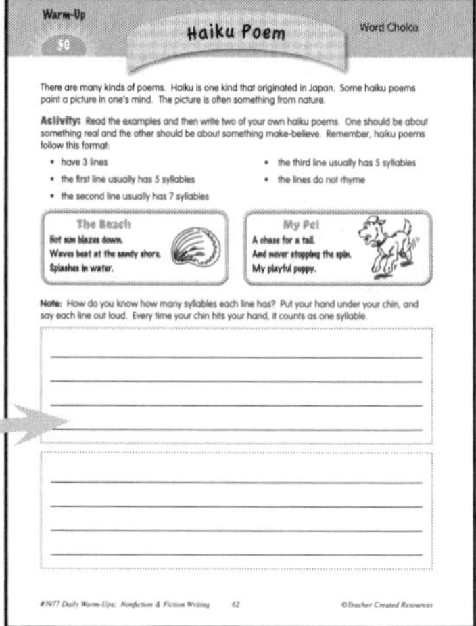
Warm-Up
50
Haiku Poem
Word Choice

There are many kinds of poems. Haiku is one kind that originated in Japan. Some haiku poems paint a picture in one's mind. The picture is often something from nature.

Activity: Read the examples and then write two of your own haiku poems. One should be about something real and the other should be about something make-believe. Remember, haiku poems follow this format:

- have 3 lines
- the first line usually has 5 syllables
- the second line usually has 7 syllables
- the third line usually has 5 syllables
- the lines do not rhyme

The Beach
Hot sun blazes down.
Waves beat at the sandy shore.
Splashes in water.

My Pet
A chase for a tail.
And never stopping the spin.
My playful puppy.

Note: How do you know how many syllables each line has? Put your hand under your chin, and say each line out loud. Every time your chin hits your hand, it counts as one syllable.

Space has been provided for students to write their responses on the activity page. For instances in which students need additional space to complete an activity, use the back of the page, or continue on separate paper. Encourage students to use a notebook where they can extend their writing or create new writing pieces if they choose to do so.

The last section of the book includes a set of writing prompts that can be used throughout the year. These provide ideas, story starters, and a variety of scenarios for students to use as prompts. Students (or the teacher) can select one prompt a week to use as a topic for their writing. As an alternative, select a prompt and ask students to focus on one or two specific traits as they write. There are many ways to use these prompts. Choose a method that works best for you and your students.

Good Writing Traits

Ideas and Content

This trait lays the foundation for other aspects of effective student writing. Students need to learn to develop and organize their ideas and present them clearly. Students should gather their ideas, as well as research, seek new knowledge, and organize their information, before they begin to write. Successful writers write about what they know, the subjects in which they have expertise, or specific knowledge and experience.

In practicing the characteristics of this trait, students identify topics about which they have prior knowledge, investigate and explore topics further by conducting additional research if needed, and learn to connect their writing to their own experiences.

Writing that is strong in content includes interesting, relevant, specific details and a development of the piece as a whole. Students should have opportunities to practice organizing their ideas, writing about their own experiences, using examples and details, and writing complete pieces. This allows them to use insight and understanding to show readers what they know.

Word Choice

Paying attention to word choice enables students to write effectively so the reader will understand and want to read. Elements of the word-choice trait include using strong visual imagery and descriptive writing.

Writers learn to use accurate and precise words to say exactly what they want to communicate. Specific words convey distinct meanings. Students should use action words, as well as descriptive nouns and adjectives, to give their writing energy.

Using effective word choice implies a familiarity with the language as students learn to use parts of speech and subject-verb agreement properly. An effective writer listens to how words sound, using words that sound natural and add to the meaning of the writing.

As students become more adept at choosing the right words to express their intent, their written communication will be more easily understood and enjoyable to read.

Fluency

As students learn to incorporate the trait of fluency in their writing, they should continue to practice what they learned about the word-choice trait. As writers develop fluency, they play with different word patterns and use words to match the mood of their writing. Fluent writing contains sentences varying in length and structure.

Students should learn to express themselves in clear sentences that make sense. This will happen as they incorporate natural rhythm and flow in their writing, making sure that ideas begin purposefully and connect to one another.

A writer may engage in a process of thinking that begins by asking the question, "What if?" One question leads to another, and the writer begins to develop smooth transitions and pacing. Mastery of each component of the fluency trait leads to a final outcome—the ability to pass a read-aloud test.

As students learn about the fluency trait, they should practice ways to express themselves by writing in a variety of formats. They will gather words to create word patterns and match specific moods.

Good Writing Traits *(cont.)*

Voice

As students gain confidence using the trait of fluency, they begin to learn about writing style. The voice trait focuses specifically on a writer's individual style. An effective piece of writing that exhibits aspects of the voice trait will sound like a particular person wrote it. Therefore, writing that has characteristics of voice will also be fluent; it will have natural rhythm. Authors develop their own unique style by writing from their thoughts and feelings. An author's personality comes through in his or her writing. Effective writers focus on their audience—they write to the reader. They want to call attention to the writing and draw the reader in. To do this, authors will write honestly, sincerely, and with confidence. As they write based on their own experiences and knowledge of themselves, writers will have the ability to bring a topic to life.

Students should continue to practice expanding their perspectives, as well as read sample pieces written from another person's point of view. By doing so, they will learn to identify elements of the voice trait in written samples and begin to develop their own style by writing reflections and personal correspondence.

Organization

Once students learn to incorporate the organization trait in their writing, they begin to view the whole picture. Effective writing has a logical order and sequence with clear direction and purpose; it does not confuse the reader. Rather, writing that displays qualities of organization guides the reader through the writing, leading to the main point. Writers who incorporate the characteristics of the organization trait include an introduction that captures the reader's attention and conclude the piece by making the reader think. Organized writing flows smoothly, with transitions that tie together.

Students can practice the characteristics of this trait by learning about beginnings and endings of stories and paragraph structure. They should practice writing their own paragraphs. The teacher can assist by introducing story elements to the students and giving them opportunities to outline a story, identify story elements, and write a complete story. As students learn to organize their written work, they begin to focus on appropriate pacing and transitions in their writing, leading to a more cohesive and readable final product.

Conventions

Students put the pieces together as they worked through the organization trait and began to consider the whole picture. They also had opportunities to consider self-evaluation, based on established criteria. The next major step in the writing process is editing. The conventions trait breaks the huge task of editing into smaller parts—allowing students to practice editing their own and others' work, focusing on one factor at a time.

Students learn about and practice correct forms of conventions such as correctly spelling plural and singular forms of nouns, capitalization of place names, punctuation, possessives, and subject-verb agreement. While students often practice characteristics of the conventions trait by reading and editing samples written by others, it is important that they continually edit their own work.

Presentation

The trait of presentation refers to the publication part of the writing process. After students have completed a written piece, they present it to their audience: visually, orally, or using both formats. The presentation trait consists of two components: visual and auditory.

Students consider appropriate visual formats for their writing, as well as the use of color. Visual aids include charts, diagrams, and graphs. The visuals may include text. Specifically, students learn how to create a graph for a presentation.

The auditory component of presentation includes presenting work in an oral format; students learn public-speaking skills through drama and critique. Practicing this trait also gives students the opportunity to speak about personal experiences, ask and respond to questions, and clearly state their main points when presenting their writing to others.

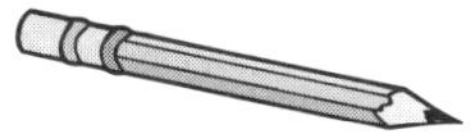

A NOTE ABOUT PRESENTATION

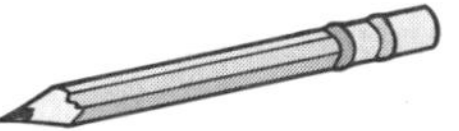

While presentation is not included among the sections of this book, it should still be considered an important trait. The goal of the activities in this book is to provide relatively short, daily warm-up practice. The presentation process involves additional time and preparation. However, you can periodically allow students to display and present some of their writing to an audience with a focus on good visual and auditory techniques.

EVALUATING THE EFFECTIVE USE OF TRAITS IN THE WRITING WARM-UPS

A sample scoring rubric is provided on page 8. Each trait can be presented individually so that it can be used to help students as they first learn about the Good Writing Traits, or page 8 can be passed out in its entirety to serve as a reference.

Use each rubric trait by itself to score writing from that section or combine traits to match special assignments. You can also teach the traits in a cumulative manner, adding one trait to your rubric as you begin each section. Another option is to create your own descriptions using page 8 as an example. Yet another alternative is to include students in the process by creating a rubric with them based on their growing understanding of each trait.

Before using any rubric, make sure students are aware of the criteria for which they will be assessed. Model sample writing pieces using the trait and criteria prior to using the rubric as a tool for evaluation. Keep in mind that a rubric is flexible and can be adapted for specific writing practice or group warm-ups. It is an effective and relatively quick way to assess student progress.

Sample Scoring Rubric

	4	3	2	1
Ideas and Content	The writing has a clear central idea, and it is supported by vivid details.	The writing has a clear central idea, but it doesn't have many details supporting it.	The writing has a developing central idea; details may be focused on another idea.	The writing does not have a clear central idea; there are not enough details, or the details are not related.
Word Choice	The writer chose the most clear and engaging words for the meaning and purpose.	The meaning is clear, and some of the writer's word choices are engaging and match the purpose.	While the meaning is clear, the vocabulary is very basic or is not a good choice for the purpose.	Words are used incorrectly, or the vocabulary is too limited to show the meaning.
Fluency	Sentence length is varied, and the writing flows well.	The writing is readable, and in some parts, the writing flows well.	The writing is readable but does not flow.	The writing can be read aloud only with practice.
Voice	The tone is engaging, and the writing was thoughtfully created for a specific audience.	The writing was obviously intended for a specific audience.	The writing is generic; it is not engaging, and it may not be clear who the intended audience is.	The writing is not appropriate for the audience.
Organization	The writing is organized clearly, and it logically moves the reader through the text.	The writing is organized; the structure makes sense, though there are better alternatives.	There was an attempt at organization, but the writing would make more sense in another structure.	There is no clear structure. Events and information seem random.
Conventions	Appropriate conventions make the writing clear and readable. Errors are few.	The writer has control of the basic conventions. There are some errors, but they are not distracting.	The writer has made some mistakes consistently throughout. Errors are distracting.	Errors make the writing difficult to read. The writer incorrectly uses basic conventions.
Presentation	The writing is neat, and the visual elements add appeal. If read aloud, it is read in a practiced, engaging manner.	The writing is neat and readable. The visual elements are not distracting.	The writing is readable. It can be read aloud clearly.	Presentation is distracting or messy, making the meaning unclear.

Standards for Writing

Each activity in *Daily Warm-Ups: Nonfiction & Fiction Writing* meets at least one of the following standards and benchmarks, which are used with permission from McREL. Copyright 2012 McREL. Mid-continent Research for Education and Learning, 4601 DTC Boulevard, Suite 500, Denver, Colorado 80237. Telephone: 303-337-0990. Website: *www.mcrel.org/standards-benchmarks*. To align McREL Standards to the Common Core Standards, go to *www.mcrel.org*.

Uses the general skills and strategies of the writing process

1. Prewriting: Uses prewriting strategies to plan written work (e.g., uses graphic organizers, story maps, and webs; groups related ideas; takes notes; brainstorms ideas; organizes information according to type and purpose of writing)

3. Editing and Publishing: Uses strategies to edit and publish written work (e.g., edits for grammar, punctuation, capitalization, and spelling at a developmentally appropriate level; uses reference materials; excludes extraneous details and inconsistencies; selects presentation format according to purpose; uses available technology to publish work)

5. Uses strategies (e.g., adapts focus, organization, point of view; determines knowledge and interests of audience) to write for different audiences (e.g., self, peers, teachers, adults)

6. Uses strategies (e.g., adapts focus, point of view, organization, form) to write for a variety of purposes (e.g., to inform, entertain, explain, describe, record ideas)

7. Writes expository compositions (e.g., identifies and stays on the topic; develops the topic with simple facts, concrete details, examples, definitions, quotations, and explanations; uses domain-specific or content area vocabulary; excludes extraneous and inappropriate information; uses logical organizing structures such as cause-and-effect, chronology, similarities and differences; uses several sources of information; provides a concluding statement)

8. Writes narrative accounts, such as poems and stories (e.g., establishes a context that enables the reader to imagine the event or experience; develops characters, setting, and plot; creates an organizing structure; uses transitions to sequence events; uses concrete sensory details; uses strategies such as dialogue, tension, and suspense; uses an identifiable voice)

9. Writes autobiographical compositions (e.g., provides a context within which the incident occurs, uses simple narrative strategies, and provides some insight into why this incident is memorable)

10. Writes expressive compositions (e.g., expresses ideas, reflections, and observations; uses an individual, authentic voice; uses narrative strategies, relevant details, and ideas that enable the reader to imagine the world of the event or experience)

11. Writes in response to literature (e.g., summarizes main ideas and significant details; relates own ideas to supporting details; advances judgments; supports judgments with references to the text, other works, other authors, nonprint media, and personal knowledge)

12. Writes personal letters (e.g., includes the date, address, greeting, body, and closing)

Standards for Writing *(cont.)*

Uses the stylistic and rhetorical aspects of writing

1. Uses descriptive and precise language that clarifies and enhances ideas (e.g., concrete words and phrases, common figures of speech, sensory details)
2. Uses paragraph form in writing (e.g., indents the first word of a paragraph, uses topic sentences, recognizes a paragraph as a group of sentences about one main idea, uses an introductory and concluding paragraph, writes several related paragraphs)
3. Uses a variety of sentence structures in writing (e.g., expands basic sentence patterns, uses exclamatory and imperative sentences)

Uses grammatical and mechanical conventions in written compositions

1. Writes in cursive
2. Uses pronouns in written compositions (e.g., substitutes pronouns for nouns, uses pronoun agreement)
3. Uses nouns in written compositions (e.g., uses plural and singular naming words, forms regular and irregular plurals of nouns, uses common and proper nouns, uses nouns as subjects, uses abstract nouns)
4. Uses verbs in written compositions (e.g., uses a wide variety of action verbs, past and present verb tenses, simple tenses, forms of regular verbs, verbs that agree with the subject)
5. Uses adjectives in written compositions (e.g., indefinite, numerical and predicate adjectives; uses conventional patterns to order adjectives)
6. Uses adverbs in written compositions (e.g., to make comparisons)
7. Links ideas using connecting words (e.g., uses coordinating conjunctions in written compositions)

9. Uses conventions of spelling in written compositions (e.g., spells high-frequency, commonly misspelled words from appropriate grade-level list; uses a dictionary and other resources to spell words; uses initial consonant substitution to spell related words; uses vowel combinations for correct spelling; uses contractions, compounds, roots, suffixes, prefixes, and syllable constructions to spell words)
10. Uses conventions of capitalization in written compositions (e.g., titles of people; proper nouns [names of towns, cities, counties, and states; days of the week; months of the year; names of streets; names of countries; holidays]; first word of direct quotations; heading, salutation, and closing of a letter)
11. Uses conventions of punctuation in written compositions (e.g., uses periods after imperative sentences and in initials, abbreviations, and titles before names; uses commas in dates and addresses and after greetings and closings in a letter; uses apostrophes in contractions and possessive nouns; uses quotation marks around titles and with a comma for direct quotations; uses a colon between hour and minutes; use commas for tag questions, direct address, and to set off words)

Ideas and Content

Shark Skin

If you rub your hand on shark skin, you may bleed because shark skin has many little teeth in it. These little teeth are called *denticles.*

Shark skin was used to smooth wood before sandpaper was invented. Today, shark skin can have its denticles removed. Then it is made into shoes. The shoes can last four times longer than other leather shoes!

Activity: A pair of shark skin shoes is for sale. They are two times the price of other shoes. Your friend says, "They aren't worth it. They can't be shark skin because they are smooth."

Explain why the shoes may or may not be shark skin. Then indicate whether you think they are a good or poor buy for you or for others. When you write, think about price, fashion, foot size, hand-me-downs, and time.

Slipping Swords

IMAGINE THAT!

Long ago, warriors in Japan wrapped shark skin around their sword handles. The rough skin kept their hands from slipping.

Activity: Write about a young boy in Japan long ago. Imagine that the boy is not as strong as other boys or warriors, so everyone laughs at him. Imagine that all the warriors had problems with swords slipping out of their hands. Describe what happens when the boy figures out a way to keep his sword from slipping!

Shark Teeth

Activity: Compare your teeth to shark teeth. Use some of the information from the Shark Tooth Fact Box when you write.

Shark Tooth Fact Box

- 5 to 15 rows of teeth in each jaw
- teeth not set firmly into jaw
- tooth lasts about a week
- tooth may be lost every time shark bites into something
- when tooth is lost, tooth behind it moves forward
- sometimes new tooth is lost in less than 24 hours!
- sharks replace teeth all their lives
- teeth grow bigger as shark grows bigger
- different sharks have different-shaped teeth

The Missing Teeth

Activity: Write a story using this basic plot:

- A child loses three or more teeth at once.
- The teeth have gone missing.
- The child is upset because he or she thinks the teeth need to be glued back in his or her mouth.

Develop the content of your story by adding details such as the child's name and age. Did he or she know the teeth were loose? Was he or she afraid to have them pulled? Are they stuck in an apple, gum, sticky candy, or a carrot stick? Were the teeth found? How was the child calmed down?

Grim's Swim

Newspapers are full of stories called *articles*. People read articles for facts. The title of an article is called a *headline*. A headline should make someone want to read the story. Important articles have *bylines*, which name the writers of the articles.

Activity: Use the information from the Idea Box to write an article. Include a headline and your byline.

Idea Box

- great white shark named Grim
- attracted to boat with tuna bait
- when close, tag stuck under shark's skin with long pole
- Grim tracked on 1,500 mile trip
- starts, returns to New Zealand
- returns less than a mile from where left!
- proved by tracking satellite tag
- sharks have organs that sense heat, pressure, and electric fields
- sharks navigate in response to ocean currents and Earth's electromagnetic field

____

By: ______________________________

Shark Tourist

IMAGINE THAT!

Imagine that you are a newspaper reporter. You are assigned to write an article on a new type of tourism, in which tourists pay to go into the ocean in a cage. Great white sharks surround the cage and sometimes charge it! The sharks come because people in the boat throw out bait.

Activity: Write your article, describing what you did or saw and how you felt. Make your story exciting to read. Then add a paragraph in which you discuss your thoughts about this kind of tourism. Finally, write a headline (title) that grabs the reader's attention.

____

By: ______________________________

Something Wrong

What is wrong with this story?

> *Laurie was walking on the beach. Suddenly, she saw something poking out of the sand. It was a hard, white bone! Laurie dug up the sand around the bone, and what did she find? More bones! Laurie had found an entire skeleton of a great white shark!*
>
> **Hint:** Sharks do not have one bone in their bodies.

When writers write, they use what they know. If they don't know something, they ask questions and do research. They investigate a topic using as many resources as possible.

If the writer had done his or her research, the writer would have known that a shark's skeleton is not made of bone. It is made of cartilage, which is soft and flexible. Your nose has cartilage!

Activity: Choose a real topic. It could be an animal, a famous landmark, or even a country. Then write a paragraph in which some of the information is incorrect. Perhaps a country is on the wrong continent or an animal has spots when it should have stripes. On the back of this page, write the incorrect content of the story. Have other people read your paragraph. Did they notice what was wrong?

The Alibi

You are a detective who is talking to a suspect about a crime you think he or she may have committed. The suspect says, "I didn't do it. I have an alibi. My alibi is that I was at the game."

Activity: What type of game did the suspect attend? You choose. Then write a paragraph to finish the suspect's alibi. Include several details about the game that you know to be incorrect. In a second paragraph, have the detective explain why the suspect's alibi is untrue.

Stomach Surprise

Many surprising things have been found inside shark stomachs. What are some of the things? The list includes a fur coat, license plates, and a barrel of nails. Rubber boots, raincoats, tablecloths, and tin cans are also on the list.

Activity: Think of a time in your own life when you were surprised or when you discovered something almost unbelievable. Tell where and when it happened and explain why it was surprising. If you can, tell how or why it happened.

Lost and Found

Activity: Write a story in which you or another character lose something. Make sure that the lost item is labeled with a name and address so it can be traced. In the story, have someone contact you or the character, revealing that the lost item has been found inside a shark!

When you write, include many details. Describe the lost item and tell how, when, and where it was lost. Tell how you or the person who lost it felt. It is your story—you can decide how long it is before the lost item is returned. Is it months or years? Who found the shark, and where was it found? Why or how was it caught? Don't forget to include a title!

Title:

News Interview

Part of a news reporter's job is to interview people. The reporter will think of questions ahead of time. This helps reporters find out what they want to know, and it keeps the conversation flowing.

Activity: Write a news interview between you and a marine biologist. The marine biologist you are interviewing studies sharks. Use the ideas in the box below, or think of your own, to help you write questions you could ask. Think of some possible answers, too.

First, greet your audience. Then introduce yourself and your guest. Include words and phrases that make the conversation flow. Remember to put a colon (:) after the name of the person who is speaking. (You can make up any name you want for the biologist.)

- interest in marine biology
- first shark experience
- favorite shark story
- fact and fiction about sharks

Interview with a Hero

IMAGINE THAT!

Imagine that it is the future. You have a radio or television talk show, and you are interviewing someone. The person is someone you admire or consider to be your hero.

Activity: Record the dialogue between you and the person. When you write, remember to introduce yourself to the audience. Tell them who you are interviewing. Explain to the audience why this person is your hero or why you admire him or her. Ask questions and make up answers. Remember to separate the name of the person speaking from what he or she says with a colon (:).

Detective Training

Have you ever thought about being a detective? You might need to remember the details of an investigation. For example, what were people wearing? What size shoes did they wear? What colors were their eyes? How did they seem? How did they walk? How did they spend their time?

Activity: Write a paragraph or two about someone you know. Include many rich details in your description. Write about his or her likes and dislikes. Discuss how the person spends his or her time and with whom.

Example sentences with details:

Tara has long, blond hair that falls about four inches down her back.

Jason leans forward a bit when he walks. He tends to pass people in the hall.

Cora often wears faded blue jeans and striped t-shirts.

Spy Glance

IMAGINE THAT!

Imagine you are a spy. You have to quickly look in a room or at a drawing of a room and then memorize where everything is. Later, you will be asked to recall the number and location of windows and doors. You will be asked about color, furniture, and other items.

Activity: Practice being a spy by thinking of a room. It can be your classroom, another room in the school, or a room in your house. Describe the room in full detail, including its size, color, and location. Record possible entry and exit points, what is in it, and where items are located. Also mention possible hiding places for something the size of a shoe box.

> **Example:** *The clock was the size and shape of a dinner plate. It was on the north-facing wall to the left of the door.*

Out-of-Town Guests

People will often have out-of-town guests who are relatives or friends. When you have guests, you are the host. As a host, you want to keep your guests busy and happy. You know your community better than anyone. To entertain guests, where can you take them or what can you do together?

Activity: Write a letter to a possible guest you might have. Think of the age of your guest. Then describe some activities you can do together. Explain why the person might enjoy doing these activities. Plan for a two-day visit, using one paragraph to describe each day.

Dear ______________________,

The CN Tower

The CN Tower is in Toronto, Canada. It has 181 stories and contains a restaurant that is over 1,000 feet above the ground. As people eat, the floor circles around the tower.

People can walk across a glass floor and look down at the streets far below their feet. The glass floor is $2\frac{1}{2}$ inches thick. Some people get dizzy or feel ill when looking down. Tests are done on the floor every year to make sure it is safe.

People can also dare to take the EdgeWalk, which takes place 1,168 feet above the ground in the open! One is harnessed to a rail and allowed to walk around the top of the tower on a five-foot ledge. Some people dare to lean out and have nothing underneath them as they look over the edge!

Activity: Imagine you are going to Toronto to visit a friend. Write a letter to your friend, expressing that you do or do not want to go to the CN Tower. Describe what you might or might now want to do at the tower, and explain why you feel this way.

Dear ______________________________,

____

____

____

____

____

____

____

____

____

____

How to Get Ready

Activity: You know how to get ready for school. What if you needed to teach someone else? Write a "how-to" on how to get ready for school, breaking it down into steps. Decide if you will start the night before or in the morning when school starts. When you write, think about homework, clothes, bathing, teeth, food, and school supplies. Also think about time. Write a title for your "how-to" and number all of your steps.

Title:

52 + 49

Imagine that an alien comes to the classroom. This problem is written on the board:

When you add fifty-two to forty-nine, what is the sum?

The alien does not know what to do at all. The alien says, "Where are the numbers? I don't see any numbers! What is the sum? Don't you want the answer?"

Activity: Write a "how-to" for the alien that explains what to do. Give your writing a title and number your steps. In your "how-to," make sure you include steps in which you explain what the sum is and how to write the problem in number form. Add a step in which you explain that you can choose how the problem is written out. You can write it out with one number above the other, in a line, or in word form. For example: 14 + 11 = 25, or fourteen plus eleven equals twenty-five.

Title:

Roping Around

Advertisers want you to buy their products. Some advertisers use examples to demonstrate how the products can be used. For example, a scooter manufacturer may show children riding their scooters on a path.

Activity: What would you include if you were writing an ad for a basic jump rope? You would need to come up with some examples of how the rope could be used. Include interesting and entertaining details with your examples.

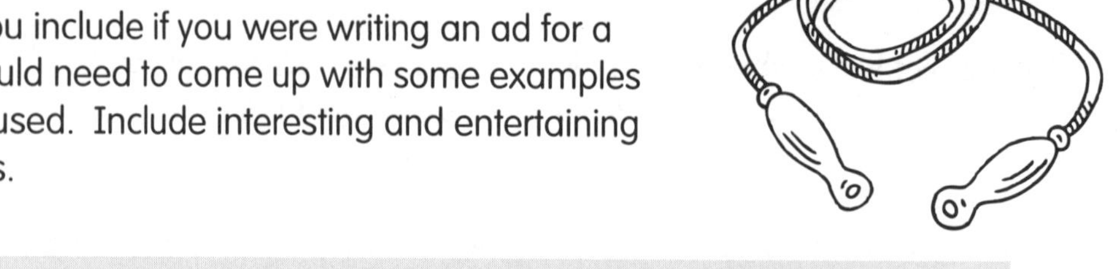

Example: *You are riding your bike along a steep mountain path. You have a backpack on. You're not worried about the cliffs or the altitude. Your only worry is the backpack strap that has broken. Then you pull out your trusty jump rope. You use the rope to tie the broken strap together!*

You're Selling What?

In 1943, Richard James was working on a project for Navy ships. He dropped a tension spring. When he saw it moving back and forth, he thought he could make a toy. It took two years, but he eventually made the Slinky. The name comes from a Swedish word that means "sleek." Ads showed children playing with the toy on stairs.

Activity: Imagine that you invented something. It can be a toy, a tool, or anything else. Decide on a name for it. Then write down some examples of how it can be used. Include details with your examples. Add a title for your invention story.

Title:

Crocodile Journal

Scientists study animals in the wild. They keep journals or diaries about what they see. They give details about what the animals eat and do, how they grow, and their surroundings.

Activity: Write three journal entries for a scientist watching crocodiles. Make the entries for different life stages. Describe what the scientist learns. Use the Crocodile Fact Box to help you think about how much time you should have between entries.

Crocodile Fact Box

- one of the few reptiles to protect young
- cow (female croc) builds mound or digs hole
- lays 35 to 40 eggs
- stays nearby, guarding for 72 to 92 days
- hears babies grunting when ready to hatch and gently bites egg so it will open easily
- carries hatchlings (baby crocs) to water in mouth!
- guards for first year
- babies will crawl on mother's back or in mouth for protection

Date: ____________________

____

____

____

Date: ____________________

____

____

____

Date: ____________________

____

____

____

The Cow that Didn't Eat

Activity: Write two diary entries. In the first entry, write with excitement about a child who is going to see a cow that:

- hasn't eaten for many months.
- stores fat in its tail.
- will grow all of its life.

In the second entry, have the child tell that he or she did not see a dairy cow. Tell how he or she learned that female crocodiles are called *cows*.

For both entries, include what you think the child is thinking and how he or she feels.

A Changing World

The world is always changing. New inventions change how things are done. For example, X-rays today are quite common. Doctors use them to check for broken bones and for foreign objects. Yet when the first X-rays were taken, people were afraid. Some people fainted when they saw X-ray pictures! It was in 1896 that the first X-rays were used to help set a boy's broken arm.

Activity: Think of an invention that has changed the way people do things. It can be significant or minor. Then write how this invention has helped to change the world. Include what you think it was like before the invention, and then explain how things are done now. Add your thoughts about whether the invention will be changed or improved in the future. Use examples from your own life.

Invention:

Jumping Boots

Imagine that jumping boots have been invented. With jumping boots, you can leap into the air. Write a story about a day when you wear jumping boots. It is your story, so you can decide how far you can travel with each leap and how high you can jump into the air.

Activity: Fill your story with details about what you see and do. You can use your own life to help write this story. For example, you can tell about an activity done with your friends or going to school. It is just a little different when using the jumping boots!

Cinquain

DID YOU KNOW?

A cinquain (pronounced *sing-cane*) is a kind of poem. A cinquain poem describes a noun, or a person, place, thing, or idea. Cinquain poems have five lines and are usually unrhymed.

Activity: Write two cinquain poems following the format below. One poem should be about something real. The other one should be about something make-believe.

Title (same as first line)

Line 1: one noun (person, place, thing, or idea)

Line 2: two adjectives (words that describe)

Line 3: three verbs (action words that end with -ing)

Line 4: phrase or sentence about the title

Line 5: one word that renames your title

Example 1 — NonFiction	Example 2 — Fiction
Shark Shark Strong, powerful Swimming, hunting, devouring Funny that, like a dog, its babies are called pups King	**Badabing** Badabing Strange, thirsty Sipping, slurping, guzzling Odd that an alien came for a drink Visitor
__________ __________ __________ __________ __________ __________ __________	__________ __________ __________ __________ __________ __________ __________

Word Choice

Tired or Exhausted?

If one is tired or exhausted, one lacks energy and may want to go to sleep or rest. Which word should a writer use: tired or exhausted? Does it matter? Yes, it does matter. This is because the writer can set a mood and help the reader feel a certain way. The writer can help the reader form a better picture in his or her head. *Exhausted* makes one think of more than just being tired. It makes one think that one can barely move.

Activity: Look at the action word pairs. Decide which action in each pair best describes *tired* or *exhausted* compared to the other action. Write each answer in the correct column.

a. ran up a hill **or** ran 15 miles

b. swam 10 hours **or** swam 10 minutes

	tired	exhausted
a.		
b.		

Activity: Think of a time in your life when you were tired. Then think of a time in your life when you were exhausted. Write two paragraphs in which you describe these times, using many details. Tell what you were doing and how you felt. You can be doing different things, or you can be doing the same thing but for a longer amount of time.

Sad, Sad, Sad

Activity: Think of all the words and phrases you can use to say or show that someone is sad. Write some of them in the box.

Activity: Now write a story in which you use some of these words and phrases. In your story, have someone think that everyone has forgotten his or her birthday. The person keeps hoping that someone will remember, but no one does, so the person gets sadder and sadder. Finally, at the end, there is a surprise party! No one had forgotten after all!

Job on Mount Washington

Think of an advertisement you have seen or read recently. Words in ads are chosen carefully. Some ads are for jobs. Businesses want people to work for them so they write ads in order to attract the most qualified people.

Mount Washington is in New Hampshire. There is a weather station on top of it. The station is in need of another meteorologist to work there. (Meteorologists study weather and the climate.) Below are some job facts for a meteorologist at Mount Washington.

- rise at 4:00 a.m.
- cook, clean, use and repair computers
- live at station with few other people (but there are visits from media and educational groups)
- measure wind, rain, snow, temperature
- have to go outside all year
- average 102 inches of rain per year
- average 310 inches of snow per year
- second-highest surface wind of 231 mph here!
- chop off ice from ladders and climb
- write and give forecast on radio
- help rescue lost, freezing hikers

Activity: Write a job advertisement for a meteorologist at Mount Washington. Remember, you have to make the job sound appealing because you want people to apply! Use words that describe the job in a positive light.

A Must Read

What if you want someone to read a book? You do not say the book is "okay." You say it is "fantastic" or a "page turner." You say the plot was "gripping" and the characters were "unforgettable." You say the book is a "must read."

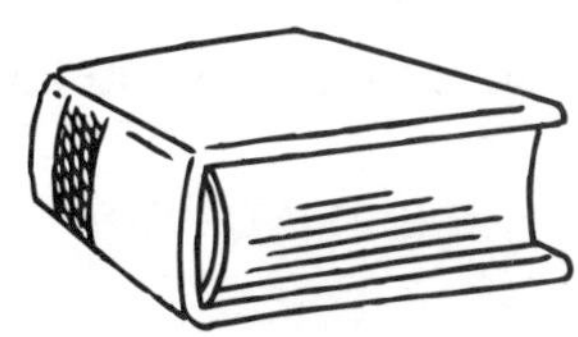

Activity: Make up a book title that will grab the reader's attention. Think about what type of book it is (action, scary, funny, mystery, etc.) and then write an advertising paragraph for it. Use words that will make people want to read the book. In your ad, describe how people will feel or what they will find when they read. Make the reader want to buy the book to find out what happens.

Surviving the Sandstorm

In the sentence pairs below, one sentence in each pair helps you form a better picture in your head. Which sentences do you think do this?

a. The sun was hot. **b.** The sun blistered down.

a. Jay felt the heat. **b.** Jay was blasted by the heat.

Writers use words such as *blistered* and *blasted* to help readers sense or feel what is happening. The words make their writing more interesting.

Mauro Prosperi was a runner who was in a six-day race across the Sahara Desert. When a sandstorm struck, Mauro got lost. He spent nine days searching for help and struggling for survival. He drank dew off of some leaves and ate bats, scorpions, lizards, and snakes. When he was found, he had lost nearly 40 pounds of body weight!

Activity: Write a paragraph about how Mauro might have felt during and after the sandstorm. Use words that help the reader feel and sense what Mauro experienced.

Surviving the Desert

Activity: Write a story with a surprise ending. In your story, include two characters. One character tells the other about surviving in the desert, but the character does not mention heat or the sun. Instead, the character talks about ice, wind, and cold. Only at the end does the other character discover that the desert is Antarctica! Antarctica is a cold desert that is very dry. The average precipitation (water from the sky) is about two inches per year.

When you write, use words that will help the reader feel how cold and windy Antarctica is. Describe blowing ice, which stings, stabs, and cuts!

English Lesson

It is hard to learn English. This is because many words can be used in more than one way. For example, the word *tie* can be used to describe something a man wears around his neck, or it can be used to tell someone to form a knot in his or her shoelaces.

Activity: Write a dialogue that can be used to teach English language learners about sound words and their other meanings. Words that sound like the said words are called *onomatopoeia.* Use some of the onomatopoeic words in the box or think of your own. Look at the example to help you begin.

buzz	**bang**	**honk**	**plop**	**woof**	**hiss**

Student: Dogs bark.

Teacher: Yes, but you can bark out an answer when you are feeling angry.

Student: Lions roar.

Teacher: Yes, but ____________________

Student: ____________________

Teacher: ____________________

Student: ____________________

Teacher: ____________________

Student: ____________________

Teacher: ____________________

Student: ____________________

Teacher: ____________________

Student: ____________________

Teacher: ____________________

Student: ____________________

Teacher: ____________________

The Right Time

Word Choice

Activity: Write a dialogue between two people. The first person says it is the right time to learn the difference between an alligator and a crocodile. The other person keeps saying it isn't the right time because it is time to go. At the end, have the second person explain why. There is a huge alligator or crocodile creeping up on them! Include facts in your dialogue.

Shape of Jaw	Fourth Tooth (Lower Jaw)
Alligator: wide, U-shaped, rounded snout	**Alligator:** covered when mouth closed
Crocodile: longer, V-shaped, more pointed snout	**Crocodile:** sticks up over upper lip

Flying Baby

Below are two headlines for newspaper articles that talk about the same story. Think about which story you would rather read.

Baby Sleeps Through Tornado OR **Tornado Sucks Up Sleeping Baby**

Writers choose words for newspaper stories that make people want to read the stories. In the headlines above, the verbs (action words) are *sleeps* and *sucks*. *Sucks* sounds more thrilling than *sleeps*.

Activity: Choose one of the headlines above and write the article that goes with it. Use the information in the box below to write your story. In your article, use many exciting action words, and tell how you think the bystanders and the mother felt. Make your reader want to keep reading!

Who: baby sleeping in stroller

What: sleeping baby in stroller lifted 50 feet into the air; set down safely 328 feet away; baby never woke up

Where: Ancona, Italy

When: September 4, 1981

Why: tornado

____

By: ______________________________

Coming Home

IMAGINE THAT!

Imagine that you just had the wildest experience of your life. You were caught in a tsunami! Fortunately, you returned home unharmed.

Activity: Write a newspaper article about your experience. In your article, tell who, what, where, when, and why. Make people want to read your story by using a lot of action words. It is your story, so you choose the events, how long you were gone, and how you got home. Include an exciting headline.

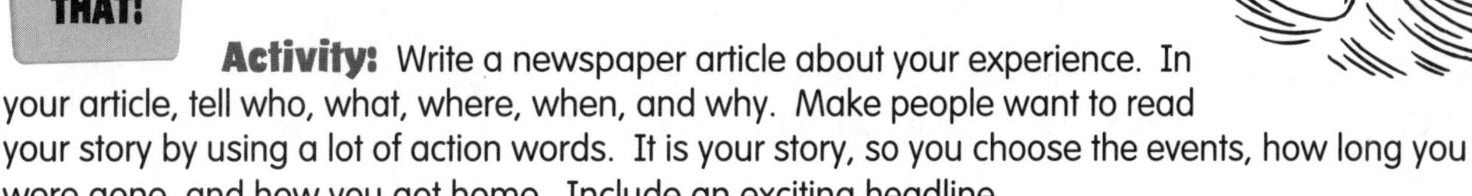

By: ______________________________

Bike Safety

Activity: Write a "how-to" for how to ride a bike safely. Be specific and write clearly so people will remember what to do. Include a title and number your steps.

Before you write, think about these things: being safe, helmets, loose clothes and backpack straps, what side of the road to ride on, and traffic.

Title:

Backpack Safety

Imagine that it is the future. You have a backpack that is unlike anything you might see today. Your backpack can make you fly! People use the backpacks the same way that we use bikes today.

Activity: Write a "how-to" for futuristic backpack safety. Be specific and write clearly so people will remember what to do. Include a title for your "how-to."

Before you write, think about these things: backpack safety (you don't want it to fall off!), how to pass someone, what to do if you meet someone in the air, how people will signal if they are going up, down, left, right, or stopping.

Title:

Hot Chili Pepper

Activity: Think of all the words you can that mean the same as *hot*. Then think of all the words you can that mean the same as *strong*. List them below.

- **hot:** ______________________________
- **strong:** ______________________________

Use as many words as you can from your list to write a paragraph in which you describe the "ghost pepper." Read the information about this chili pepper in the Fact Box before you get started.

Bhut Jolokia Chili Pepper Fact Box

- known as "ghost pepper" in the U.S.
- may be world's hottest chili pepper
- from India
- a small taste makes you sweat
- some say it is like eating scorching volcanic rocks
- in India—put in smoke bombs and smeared on fence posts
- stops wild elephants from destroying crops and crushing houses

____

____

____

____

____

____

____

____

____

____

____

The Child and the Giant

Imagine that there is a bad creature, such as a giant, ogre, dragon, or other beast that comes to a settlement (city, town, or village) and does harmful things. People try to make it leave, but no one can. Then a small child says he or she will confront the beast. The child uses the "ghost pepper"—an extremely hot chili pepper.

Activity: Write a story using the information above. Think about the characters, the problem, and the solution. Your story can be funny, scary, or serious. Use words that will help the reader imagine what things look like and what actions are taking place. Include a title for your "ghost pepper" story.

Title:

What Am I?

Activity: Think of a living thing, such as an animal or a plant. Then describe it, without naming it, in ten or more lines. Think about shape, color, and other features. Also, think about what it can do or what it is used for. As your last line, write, "What am I?" Choose your words wisely so you don't make it too easy for someone to figure out.

Write what it is on the back of this page. Then share your paper with classmates. Could they guess what you were describing?

By Touch Alone

Imagine that you are blindfolded and your friend hands you a paper bag with something in it. She asks you to reach into the bag and touch the object to figure out what it is. She tells you that you cannot look inside the bag.

Activity: Make up what the object is inside the bag. Write six detailed descriptions about what you feel when you touch this object. As your last line, write, "What am I?"

When you are done, write what someone might think this thing is if he or she only reads a few clues. You may do this on the back of this page. Then read your observations to a classmate. How many clues did they need before they knew what it was?

1. ______________________________

____

2. ______________________________

____

3. ______________________________

____

4. ______________________________

____

5. ______________________________

____

6. ______________________________

____

Like a Fish

Lynne Cox was the first person to swim around the Cape of Good Hope. She wore only a swimsuit. She braved big waves and strong currents, as well as sea snakes, barracuda, and many huge sharks. Cox did not swim in a shark cage. Instead, people in a boat and divers would watch for sharks. Near the end of the swim, everyone began to yell at Cox. They told her to swim as fast as she could. Cox sprinted for shore. When she got there, she found out a shark had come directly at her! One of the people had to shoot the shark in the dorsal fin to scare it away. The blood attracted other sharks to the area, putting her in even more danger!

Activity: Write a paragraph in which you compare Lynne Cox to a fish.

Like Steel

When writing a description, a writer might say someone is "like steel." Most likely, the writer would choose that word to make the reader think the person is strong and firm. Writers would not describe a weak person as being like steel because steel is a very strong metal.

Activity: Make up a person and write why this person is similar to five different things. The things can be animals, plants, or objects such as rubber bands or raindrops. Use words that allow readers to easily imagine this person.

> **Example:** *Blake is like steel because he is so strong. One time, Blake was swimming, and a shark tried to bite him. Blake was fine, but the poor shark needed to go to a dentist!*

Action!

Which sentences in each pair below sound as if there is more action?

a. The gorilla **pounded** its chest when it **spotted** me.
b. The gorilla **hit** its chest when it **saw** me.

a. When the rhino **charged**, I **raced** and **hid** behind the tree.
b. When the rhino **ran**, I **went** and **stood** behind the tree.

When you write, you can choose action words, or verbs, that add excitement to your writing. Selecting the right action words can help make your writing more interesting.

Activity: Write a letter to a friend or relative in which you use many action words. In your letter, write about a time you did one or more of the following: (1) **shook in fear** instead of felt nervous, (2) **leapt** instead of hopped, (3) felt your **heart pounding** and **thumping** instead of gently beating.

Dear ______________________,

____

____

____

____

____

____

____

____

____

____

____

____

Show, Don't Tell

Which sentences in each pair below sound as if there is more action?

a. Jack **tumbled** down the hill.

b. Jack **went** down the hill.

a. Jill **plopped** down on the grass.

b. Jill **sat** down on the grass.

When you write, you can choose action words, or verbs, that add excitement to your writing. Selecting the appropriate action words can help make your writing more interesting.

Activity: Imagine that you are diving deep under the water. You see huge clams and whales, enormous octopi, and other sea creatures. Write a letter to your friend about your diving adventure. Include many action verbs and descriptive words to captivate your friend!

Dear ______________________________,

____

____

____

____

____

____

____

____

____

____

____

____

It's About Time

It is two o'clock. Is it two in the morning or two in the afternoon? If it is 2:00 a.m., it is very early in the morning. If it is 2:00 p.m., it is in the afternoon.

When writers write about time, they often use other words or phrases besides *a.m.* and *p.m.* to let the reader know about the time. Words and phrases such as *sunrise, sunset, noon, midnight, at dawn, in the morning,* and *in the evening* give the reader a sense of time without reading *a.m.* and *p.m.* over and over.

Activity: Describe a typical school day. Detail your morning routine and what you do at school, after school, and at night. Record all that you do at different times without writing *a.m.* and *p.m.* Instead, choose other words that will give your reader a sense of time.

Time Mix-up

Activity: Write about a time when something went wrong. Perhaps someone missed an appointment, a train ride, or a plane flight. Or maybe someone went to see a movie at the wrong hour. Why did things go wrong? People had the wrong time! They mixed up *a.m.* and *p.m.* Remember to give your story a title.

Title:

Window View

Activity: Think of a window in your house. Record what one might see outside or what might pass by the window at different times of the day. Choose which day of the week to write about. Make four entries, describing each scene in detail. For example, if you can see a car pass by, what color, size, kind, and shape is it? Where is the sun in the sky? Provide the time for each window viewing.

Day: ______________________________

Time: ______________________

____

____

____

Time: ______________________

____

____

____

Time: ______________________

____

____

____

Time: ______________________

____

____

____

Spaceship View

We see one sunset and one sunrise each day. Astronauts on the space shuttle saw 16 sunsets and 16 sunrises each day! An astronaut would see Earth's atmosphere change from daytime blue to nighttime black in only 13 seconds! Why did space shuttle astronauts see so many sunsets and sunrises? The space shuttle whipped around Earth at 17,500 miles per hour! This meant it went around Earth every 90 minutes.

Activity: Imagine you are on the space shuttle. Record what you see outside your window at different times of the day. Make at least four entries. Decide if you want them to sound realistic or fantastical.

Time: ______________________________

____

____

____

Time: ______________________________

____

____

____

Time: ______________________________

____

____

____

Time: ______________________________

____

____

____

Haiku Poem

There are many kinds of poems. Haiku is one kind that originated in Japan. Some haiku poems paint a picture in one's mind. The picture is often something from nature.

Activity: Read the examples and then write two of your own haiku poems. One should be about something real and the other should be about something make-believe. Remember, haiku poems follow this format:

- have 3 lines
- the first line usually has 5 syllables
- the second line usually has 7 syllables
- the third line usually has 5 syllables
- the lines do not rhyme

The Beach

Hot sun blazes down.
Waves beat at the sandy shore.
Splashes in water.

My Pet

A chase for a tail.
And never stopping the spin.
My playful puppy.

Note: How do you know how many syllables each line has? Put your hand under your chin, and say each line out loud. Every time your chin hits your hand, it counts as one syllable.

Fluency

Writing in Rhyme

Dr. Seuss wrote children's books. Many of his books were written with rhymes. He wrote about a cat in the hat, Sam I am (with green eggs and ham), and a fox in socks. Rhymes can make reading entertaining. When you read or say rhymes out loud, the words seem to flow. They make a pattern that is easy to listen to or say.

Activity: Practice writing your own rhymes. Think of an animal or a person. Make up some rhyming lines about what it, he, or she looks like, wears, says, and does. Does your character meet someone or create something special? Does it climb, fall, or swim somewhere? Don't forget to include a title!

If you have trouble thinking up some rhymes, don't give up! The first book Dr. Seuss wrote and illustrated was called *And to Think That I Saw It on Mulberry Street.* The book was turned down 27 times before it was sold!

Thing One and Thing Two

Activity: Dr. Seuss wrote a book with the characters Thing One and Thing Two. Create a dialogue between your own Things One and Two. Your Things One and Two can be anything you want. For example, you can have Cow One and Cow Two or Parakeet One and Parakeet Two.

Include rhymes in your dialogue. When you are done, have your classmates be Things One and Two. Did the rhymes make the dialogue humorous?

Scorpions

Scorpions are not insects. Like spiders, they are arachnids. They have eight legs and two main body parts. All scorpions have venom and can sting. There are over 1,400 kinds, but only about 50 can cause serious harm to humans. Only two of the very dangerous kinds are found in the United States.

Scorpions are nocturnal, which means they are out at night. If you shine an ultraviolet light on a scorpion, it will glow in the dark! Scorpions give birth to live babies. The mother carries her babies around on her back. She will protect them for a while, but the babies have to watch out. If the mother gets hungry, she may eat them!

Activity: What is your opinion of scorpions? Some people find them horrible, while others find them fascinating. List all the words one might use to describe scorpions and how one might feel about them.

Likes scorpions: fascinating, ____________________________________

Does not like scorpions: horrible, ____________________________________

Activity: Write two paragraphs in which you tell how you feel about scorpions and why. Explain why others might feel the opposite and why. When you write, use words from your lists above and include scorpion facts.

Scorpion Food

Scorpions are eaten in the south of China and neighboring countries. Some say that scorpions have a "woody" taste. They recommend eating it whole—except for the tip of the tail.

Activity: Describe a scene in which someone goes to dinner at someone else's house. Scorpions are part of the meal. Describe the person's reaction. Does he or she try a scorpion?

The Statue of Liberty

When you write, you need to make sure your story makes sense. Why doesn't the story below make sense? (Hint: Two things don't make sense.)

I went with my family to St. Louis, Missouri. We visited the Statue of Liberty, which was amazing. Lady Liberty's index finger alone measures eight feet long! I liked hearing what the statue said. Lady Liberty said, "Give me your tired, your poor, your huddled masses yearning to be free."

In the above story, it sounds as if the Statue of Liberty is in St. Louis. The Statue of Liberty is in New York! Second, it sounds as if the statue is talking. The words above are from a poem on the base of the statue; they were not spoken by Lady Liberty herself!

How could you fix this story so it makes sense?

1. ______________________________

2. ______________________________

Activity: Write about a place that you visited or about something you experienced. Include two statements in your story that do not make sense. For example, it might seem that you are in a different place than the one you are talking about or that an animal or nonliving thing is actually talking. Share your story with your classmates. Could anyone tell what didn't make sense?

____

____

____

____

____

____

____

____

____

____

A Pine Tree with Apples

When you write, you need to make sure your story makes sense. Why doesn't the story below make sense? (Hint: Three things don't make sense.)

I climbed high up into the pine tree and looked down. Resting on the highest branch, I felt like I was in my own leafy world. I picked an apple and thought about how old the tree was. You can tell a tree's age by counting the rings in its stump. The tree I was in was 102 years old. I know because I had counted each and every ring!

How is it possible to pick an apple from a pine tree? Has the tree been cut down or not? If there is a stump, how can there be a tree to climb? Do pine trees have leaves?

How could you fix this story so it makes sense?

1. ______________________________

2. ______________________________

3. ______________________________

Activity: Write a story or a description in which at least one thing does not make sense. It may have to do with the wrong season or time, or it may be about something that doesn't fit or work. Use your imagination! When you are done, share your story with your classmates. Could anyone tell what didn't make sense?

____

____

____

____

____

____

____

____

____

Fire, Fire

Words can help set a mood in writing. Read each phrase below and write "cheerful" or "scary" before each one to describe its mood.

	Red flames for ruin
	Hungry flames eating the forest
	Warm crackle of burning logs
	Merry flames dancing under the night sky
	Black limbs dusted with gray ash
	Snowy white marshmallows over bright flames

The words in the lines above help set a mood. They match how the writer wants us to feel. The words *ruin, hungry, eating, black,* and *ash* make us feel that forest fires can be scary. The words *warm, crackle, merry, dancing,* and *bright* remind us of sitting cheerfully around a campfire.

Activity: Now it's your turn to write two mood poems. First, choose a kind of weather. It can be gentle rain, warm sun, or soft snowfall. Then write at least six lines, describing what it looks like, how it makes you feel, and what activities you might do in it. Your lines can be a mix of complete sentences, phrases, and individual words. The lines need to set a mood and help the reader know how you feel. Then write a second poem about the same type of weather but when it is much stronger, wilder, and fiercer.

Mood: Gentle	Mood: Wild

Jack and the Giant

In the story "Jack and the Beanstalk," Jack trades in a cow for some magic beans that grow into a beanstalk. Jack climbs up the beanstalk and discovers a hen that lays golden eggs and a magic harp—both of which he steals. These treasures belonged to a giant and, once the giant spotted the thief (Jack), he chased after him. But Jack was very quick and was able to race down the beanstalk, cut it down, and return home safely.

Activity: Write two mood poems. In the first poem, have the giant describe how he feels when he realizes that Jack has stolen from him. In the second poem, have Jack describe how he feels when the giant chases him. Each poem should have at least six lines, which can be a mix of sentences, phrases, and individual words. The lines should set a specific mood.

Shark Attack

When you write, you do not want all your sentences to be the same. You want a variety of lengths. This helps your writing flow, and it keeps your writing interesting. One way to combine two sentences into one is shown below.

> *Allison was a green sea turtle. She was attacked by a shark.*
> *Allison, a green sea turtle, was attacked by a shark.*

Activity: Combine the two sentences into one long one in the same way as the example above. Remember to include commas.

1. Allison was a shark attack victim. She lost three flippers.

   ____

2. Allison was only able to swim in circles. She could not resurface after diving.

   ____

3. Tom was a worker at Sea Turtle, Inc. Tom made a suit and fiber fin so Allison could swim straight and dive.

   ____

Activity: Now it is your turn. Write three sets of sentences about real events. Each set should have two short sentences that are combined to form one long sentence.

1. ______________________________

   ____

   ____

2. ______________________________

   ____

   ____

3. ______________________________

   ____

   ____

Turtle News

IMAGINE THAT! **Imagine that you are a reporter telling the story of Allison—the green sea turtle who lost three flippers in a shark attack.**

Activity: Record what you will say using a variety of sentence lengths. This will make the news easier to listen to and will help people pay attention. Use descriptive words that excite the reader, too. Then say your newscast out loud. Did the different sentence lengths help your report flow?

Event Facts

- There was a shark attack in 2005.
- A green sea turtle named Allison lost three flippers.
- She could only swim in circles.
- She could not resurface after diving.
- Jeff George said, "It was like paddling with only one oar."
- They tried to attach a prosthetic (artificial) flipper, but it didn't work.
- Tom Wilson used $25 worth of supplies to make a suit with a Velcro-attached plastic fin.
- Now Allison can swim straight and dive.
- Jeff George says, "She seems happy now."

Good morning, listeners. This is ____________________

Fire Safety

Activity: When information is listed or when there is a catchy phrase, it may be easier to learn and remember steps. Prepare a lesson about fire safety for younger children. Record what to do in list/poster form so it is easier for young children to learn the information.

Use the back of this page as your poster paper. Add a title that tells what your instructions are for. Then write steps that begin with the bold words in the Information Box. You can include more steps, if necessary.

Information Box

If your clothes or hair catch fire, you should **stop** walking or moving immediately. Put your palms over your face to help protect it as you **drop** to the ground and lie flat. On the ground, **roll** back and forth from stomach to back until the fire is out. The faster you can put out the flames, the less serious burns you will suffer, so practice "stop, drop, and roll" until you can do it quickly. You will want to run, but this will fuel the fire with oxygen and make the flames spread faster. If there is a blanket nearby, grab it and cover yourself as you drop.

Do you think a young child would be more likely to learn the lesson about "stop, drop, and roll" from your list/poster or from the Information Box? Explain your answer.

Stop, Drop, and Roll

Activity: Make up a story with this basic plot:

- You see an animal flee from a fire.
- The animal is saved when a quick-thinking person grabs a nearby coat or blanket, covering the animal, pushing it to the ground, and rolling it.

Before you write, plan ahead. Who comes to the rescue? What actions does the rescuer take? What words will you use to help the reader feel fear, excitement, and finally, relief when the animal is saved? Don't forget to include a title!

Title:

Country Neighbors

Where is your country? You can say where things are in multiple ways by changing your sentences. Doing this helps keep your writing from being the same and helps keep the reader interested.

Example: *Which country or body of water borders your country to the north?*

Example answers:

- *The USA, my country, is bordered to the north by Canada.*
- *The country that borders my country to the north is Canada.*
- *My country's northern neighbor is Canada.*
- *My country is the USA, and its northern border is shared with Canada.*

Activity: Now it is your turn. Practice writing different sentences by answering each question in two different ways.

1. Which country or body of water borders your country to the south?

   a. ______________________________

   b. ______________________________

2. Which country or body of water borders your country to the east?

   a. ______________________________

   b. ______________________________

3. Is your country in the Northern or Southern Hemisphere? In your answer, include the names of two other countries that are in the same hemisphere.

   a. ______________________________

   ____

   b. ______________________________

   ____

4. Is your country in the Eastern or Western Hemisphere? In your answer, include the names of two other countries that are in the same hemisphere.

   a. ______________________________

   ____

   b. ______________________________

   ____

King Arthur and the Round Table

There is a legend about King Arthur. He was a great English king with many loyal knights to serve him. King Arthur met with his knights around a round table because he did not want a table with a head. He wanted all his knights to feel they were unified rather than competitive.

Activity: Imagine that you are having a party in which you and seven other people will be sitting at a round table. Decide who will be sitting where. Then describe where five of the people will be sitting in at least two different ways. Plan ahead! Write in the names of who will be sitting where in the circular chart.

Example:

a. Chloe, my friend, will be sitting on my left.

b. To my left is Chloe who is sitting next to me and my poodle, Charlie.

1. **a.** ______________________________

   b. ______________________________

2. **a.** ______________________________

   b. ______________________________

3. **a.** ______________________________

   b. ______________________________

4. **a.** ______________________________

   b. ______________________________

5. **a.** ______________________________

   b. ______________________________

If someone read just your sentences, do you think he or she would come up with the same seating chart that you made? Write your answer in the box below.

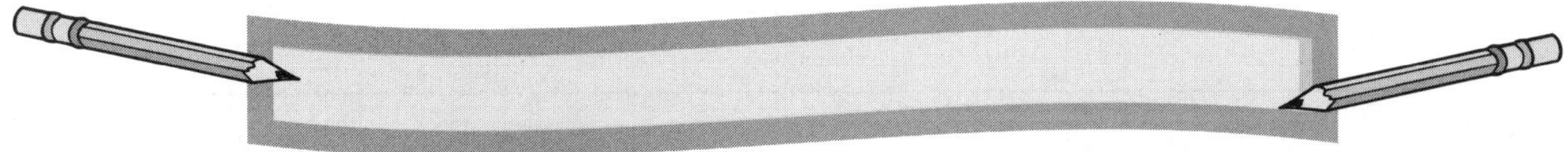

Smokejumper

Smokejumpers are a special kind of firefighter. Smokejumpers jump out of airplanes and parachute down to fires. They get there faster than anyone else. Often, they go deep into the wilderness where there is no one there to help them. They have to bring all their own supplies. Smokejumpers may meet up with bears and other wild animals, and they may not be picked up for weeks. They may have to work for hours and hours without rest.

Activity: Write an ad for a smokejumper job. Use words that would make someone want to have that job. Think of ways to make the dangers and hard work sound exciting and thrilling.

SMOKEJUMPER NEEDED

The Wrong Side

Fluency

Smokejumpers dropped to a fire in Alaska. The fire was deep in the wilderness with no roads or people nearby. They would not be picked up for many days. One smokejumper did not fight the fire. He just sat around a campfire and ate all that he wanted. Meanwhile, the other smokejumpers worked for hours without rest and had nearly empty stomachs. Why was there a smokejumper not fighting the fire? The smokejumper and most of the supplies had landed on the wrong side of the river! The river could not be crossed because it was too cold, fast, and deep.

Activity: Imagine you are a smokejumper. Write two diary entries about your job. Before you write, plan ahead. Will your entries begin before or after you parachute out of the plane? On which side of the river will you land? In your entries, write down what you do and tell how you feel. Do you like your location? How do you feel about the smokejumper(s) on the other side?

School Calendar

Not all schools have the same calendars. Some schools are open all year. They have short breaks during the year, while other schools have long breaks in the summer. What if your school was thinking about changing its calendar? What if it was thinking of doing the opposite of what it is doing now?

Activity: Write a letter to the newspaper, telling the public how you as a student feel. Plan ahead. Before you write, take your position. Share the good and positive points. Then explain why the other choice is unacceptable. If you have personal examples, include them.

Dear ______________________,

____

____

____

____

____

____

____

____

____

____

____

____

____

____

The Dog Ate My Homework

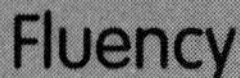

An excuse is a reason given for not doing something or not being somewhere. It is an explanation for why something did not happen. One famous excuse is that one could not do the homework because the dog ate it.

Activity: Write a letter to your teacher that contains a clever excuse. Make up a wild story in which one small thing happens that causes a chain reaction. One thing leads to another thing, and on and on. The end result is no homework. Have fun deciding what leads to what!

Note: You can have as many events in your chain reaction as you want. In your letter, remember to put the date above the greeting. End the letter with the word *Sincerely* or *Respectfully*.

____

Dear _______________,

____

____

____

____

____

____

____

New Words

Every year, new words are added to the dictionary. Many people want to know what the words are so they can write stories about them. For example, the word *mouse potato* is a noun that was first used in 1993. It came from the word *couch potato*. It is slang for a person who spends a lot of time on the computer. *Wave pool* is another new word that was first used in 1977. A wave pool is a large swimming pool with a machine for making waves. *Mouse potato* and *wave pool* were added to the 2006 dictionary.

New words are submitted to be added to the dictionary all the time. Some words are accepted, while others are rejected. To be added to the dictionary, a word has to have been in use for a long time and must be used and understood by many people.

Activity: Think of two new words that you use with your friends or family that you think should be in the dictionary. Define the words and describe how the words came about. Explain why these words should be in the dictionary. Maybe one day they will be!

For Want of a Nail

Fluency

The following is a famous nursery rhyme. It talks about how small actions can lead to big problems.

For want of a nail the shoe was lost.
For want of a shoe the horse was lost.
For want of a horse the rider was lost.
For want of a rider the battle was lost.
For want of a battle the kingdom was lost.
And all for the want of a horseshoe nail.

Activity: Write a humorous or serious story in which a small action led to a big problem. Include many details. Somewhere in your story, suggest that planning ahead might have changed the outcome. Don't forget to include a title!

Title:

Trip Plan

Activity: Plan a family vacation or a trip to a location you have always wanted to visit. Tell where you will go, when, and for how long. How will you travel there, and what will you do there? What will you need to bring? Make sure you plan ahead so you don't forget anything!

Where will you go? ______________________________

____

Who will go with you? ______________________________

____

When will you go, and for **how** long? ______________________________

____

How will you travel? ______________________________

____

____

What will you do and with **whom**? ______________________________

____

____

____

What will you need to bring? ______________________________

____

____

____

Party Planner

Fluency

There are people whose job is to plan parties. They are called "party planners." Party planners talk to the people or person who is hiring them to find out what kind of party is wanted. It may be a birthday party or a party for a big company. The party planners purchase the food and decorations and organize the games and entertainment. Some of the parties may be holiday parties, while others may be graduation parties. Some parties have themes. For example, food and decorations may be related to a specific movie or animal.

Activity: Imagine you are a party planner who is planning a party with a theme. List the steps you need to complete to make the party a success. Describe what type of food, decorations, and games you will have. Will your party be a swimming or skating party, or something else? In your title, say who the party is for. It can be for people or animals.

School Directions

Activity: Visitors are coming to your school. Provide clear directions so the visitors can get to your classroom. Tell the visitors where to park, what doors to enter, and where to find the office. Then guide them to your classroom.

When you write, use words such as *left, right, after, before, up,* and *down.* Which rooms will the visitor pass or have to walk through? Use color words if that will help, too. If your classroom is very easy to find, have the visitor go to a second location after visiting your classroom. Give directions from your classroom to the second location.

You can list the directions as numbered steps if you would like, or you can write them in paragraph form.

Telephone Directions

IMAGINE THAT! **Imagine you have left something important at home. It is hidden somewhere in a room, and your friend is going to get it for you. While you and your friend are on the phone, you must give him or her directions for locating the important item.**

Activity: Record what you will tell your friend. Tell him or her when to go *up, down, left,* or *right.* Use words such as *after* and *before.* Use color words, too, if that will help. Tell your friend how many doors to pass or which doors to go through. Make sure your friend doesn't end up in the wrong room with the wrong item!

Try to give clear instructions that can be easily understood. You can list the instructions as numbered steps if you would like, or you can write them in paragraph form.

Plan Ahead

Item to be picked up: ______________________________

Where the item is located: ______________________________

____

____

____

____

____

____

____

____

____

____

____

Devils Tower

Devils Tower is a famous natural landmark. It is a large rock sticking out of the ground in Wyoming. There are many myths about this rock. One of the myths is that seven sisters were playing when a big bear chased them. The girls ran to and climbed up a rock, which rose up like a tree. When the bear tried to reach the girls by climbing up, he slid down. The bear's claws left grooves in the rock that people can still see today. As for the girls, they are in the sky and can still be seen. They are in a group of seven stars called the Pleiades.

Activity: Now it is your turn to make up a story about a real landmark. You will have to plan ahead. First, choose your landmark and think of some true facts you will use to describe it. Then make up how the landmark came about.

Landmark Name:

Landmark Facts (Nonfiction)	How It Came About (Fiction)

Voice

Favorite Song

There are many different kinds of music in the world. Is there a special type of music you like? Do you have a favorite song?

Activity: Write a paragraph in which you describe what type of music you enjoy listening to. Name a favorite song, as well. Explain why you like this type of music and song. Do you enjoy singing along with this music or favorite song, or do you prefer to simply listen to it? How do the music and song make you feel?

Milk Music

Did you know that cows like music? Some dairy farmers pipe music into their barns. They say the music helps the cows relax and that relaxed cows give more milk. What do the farmers play? They play music that calms the cows—not rock and roll!

Activity: Imagine that you are a cow. Write down the thoughts inside your head, including how you feel about music. Is there a special song or band you like or dislike? What do you hope the farmer will play? Your response can be silly or serious. When you write, use the word *I*, as you are writing as the cow.

Park Plans

THINK ABOUT IT!

Cities plan ahead. If there is going to be a new park, they think about costs, what people need, and how much space they have.

Activity: Write a letter to the mayor of your city. Tell him or her what you want in a park. Do you want a pool or a skate park, walking or biking trails, picnic tables or sports fields? Explain to the mayor why building or including what you want would be a good use of money and space.

This is a formal letter, so include your address, the date, and the address of the city office. Close your letter with *Sincerely* or *Respectfully*. (You can make up the addresses.)

____

____

____

____

____

Dear __________________________ :

____

____

____

____

____

____

______________________________,

"Old" Plans

IMAGINE THAT! **Not all people want the same things in parks. Younger people may want a skate park, but an older person may want something else. Imagine that you are much older than you are now. Will you be a parent with young children, a teenager, or a grandparent? You choose.**

Activity: Now imagine that your city is building a new park. Write a letter to the city council from the perspective of the "older" you. Tell them who you are and what you think they should include in the new park. Tell them why building or including what you want would be a good use of money and space.

This is a formal letter, so include your address, the date, and the address of the city office. Close your letter with *Sincerely* or *Respectfully*. (You can make up the addresses.)

____

____

____

____

____

Dear ____________________:

____

____

____

____

____

____

____________________,

The Camel Law

It has been said by some that there is (or was) a silly law in Arizona that says, "One cannot hunt camels in Arizona." People consider this to be silly because camels do not roam freely in Arizona!

Activity: Write about a law that you think is silly or that needs to be changed in some way. Provide reasons as to why the law needs to be changed. Explain how you would change it to make it a better law.

I Spy a Camel

Activity: Write a dialogue between two children and a parent. The children are looking out the car windows as their parent drives through Arizona. One or both children say that they spy a camel, but the parent says it is not possible.

How will you write and end your dialogue? Will everyone see a camel? Will your dialogue have a humorous or surprise ending? It is your choice.

Shoes

Activity: Write two paragraphs about shoes. In the first paragraph, explain why shoes are used. Give examples of times in your own life when shoes have been very helpful. Describe different kinds of shoes, as well as when these different kinds of shoes are worn.

In the second paragraph, tell what you think the first shoes looked like long ago and what they were made of. Then contrast that with the shoes you are wearing now. Which shoes do you prefer?

Shoe Talk

IMAGINE THAT!

Imagine you are a shoe. What kind would you be, and who would be wearing you?

Activity: Write a paragraph in which you write as the shoe. You will use the word *I* because you are the shoe. Record your thoughts. Do you like being worn, thrown, or kicked? Do you like pavement or grass? How do you feel when the person wearing you walks or plays a game? How do you feel about being worn or being put in a closet or box?

Include emotion and feelings in your story. You can have your shoe complain or be excited about all that happens to it.

All About Teeth

Activity: Write two diary entries from the past about your teeth. You can pick how many days or years the entries are apart. Will you have lost teeth? Will you be going to the dentist? Describe your teeth and compare them to other teeth, too.

Teeth Fact Box

- They are the hardest part of any animal.
- They are most likely to be fossilized.
- Reptile teeth are replaced constantly.
- Rodents have teeth that never stop growing; they are kept sharp and short by gnawing.
- The tusks of walruses and elephants never stop growing.
- One elephant tusk weighed over 200 pounds!
- Elephants are right- or left-tusked, using one side more than the other.
- An elephant's molar can be over one foot long.

Date: ______________________

____

____

____

____

____

Date: ______________________

____

____

____

____

____

Animalcules

Antony van Leeuwenhoek was born in 1632. Van Leeuwenhoek made lenses by grinding them. When Leeuwenhoek looked through his lenses, he saw things that no one had ever seen or known about before. He called the tiny creatures *animalcules.* Today we know he saw different kinds of bacteria.

Van Leeuwenhoek once took samples of plaque. Some of the samples came from between his teeth, while others came from two old men who had never had their teeth cleaned. Van Leeuwenhoek was amazed at the number of animalcules living in his mouth, but he was shocked at the number in the mouths of the two old men.

Activity: Write down two diary entries for van Leeuwenhoek for the year 1673. Use the word *I* in your writing, as if you are him. In the entries, tell what he did and saw. Tell how he felt. Use words that make one feel surprised, amazed, and shocked.

Message in a Bottle

A message was put in a bottle that said a reward would be given to the person who returned the message. The message said to take the bottle to an address and ask for Tina. Decades later, the bottle was returned. Tina had passed away, but her daughter was still there. Tina's daughter recognized her father's handwriting. The bottle was thrown in the ocean in New Hampshire, but it was found on the island of Turks and Caicos—2,000 miles away!

Activity: Write a message for a bottle. In your message, report when and where the bottle is being set adrift. Then describe yourself. Tell what you are good at and tell what you hope to do or see in the next one, two, and three decades. (A decade is 10 years.)

Help!

IMAGINE THAT! **Imagine that you are walking on the beach in 1950. You find a very old bottle with a message inside. The message says, "Help! I am marooned on an island. My airplane went down close to Howland Island—Amelia Earhart July 4, 1937."**

Activity: Write a story explaining what you will do to try to rescue Amelia. Will you fly a plane or sail a boat? What will you bring with you? Do you find Amelia? If so, how does she and the world react? Don't forget to include a title!

Did you know that Amelia Earhart was a famous pilot? Amelia was trying to fly around the world when she disappeared. No one knows what really happened to her.

Title:

Food Poem

Not everyone likes the same foods. For example, some people may love to eat watermelon and oranges, while others may dislike eating them. Some might only like one but not the other.

Activity: Think of a food you like and then write a shape poem about it. To write a shape poem, lightly draw an outline of a food item. Then write your words along the outline. Think before you write! What will you say, and how big will your letters be?

Hint: You might want to write your poem first in pencil in case you need to adjust your word size or add or subtract words. See the example to the right.

Animal Food

IMAGINE THAT!

Imagine that you are an animal. You can be a fish, bird, insect, reptile, or mammal.

Activity: Write a food shape poem for that animal. First, think of something the animal would likely eat. Then lightly draw an outline of the food with your pencil. Write your words along the outline. Your words should describe the food from your animal's point of view. Think before you write! What will you say, and how big will your letters be?

Hint: You might want to write your poem first in pencil in case you need to adjust your word size or add or subtract words. See the example to the right.

"Why sit?" said the termite, "when I can feast on this lovely wooden chair."

Food Prep

IMAGINE THAT!

Imagine that you are teaching someone to prepare something to eat. Think of a food dish that needs to be prepared (unlike an apple that is ready to eat).

Activity: List the steps of how to prepare it. In your procedure, make sure you have a title. Include washing your hands and gathering ingredients and supplies. If you don't know the oven temperature or cooking time, just estimate. If you want the food cooked over a campfire, make sure you say so! Will you make cookies, a salad, pasta, or s'mores? You can choose any food dish.

The Alien and the Napkin

An alien comes to dinner. You have set the table. What does the alien do with its napkin? It uses it to wipe its teeth and then puts the napkin on its head! The alien clearly doesn't know what to do with it.

Activity: Write step-by-step directions for the alien, telling it what to do with its napkin. Read the information in the Napkin Rules paragraph, and then think about how to order the steps. Write the facts simply and clearly, leaving out unimportant words and including pictures when necessary.

Napkin Rules

As soon as everyone is seated, unfold your napkin and place it across your lap. If the napkin is large, keep it folded in half and place it with the fold toward you. If you need to leave the table for any reason but are coming back, place your napkin on your chair, folded loosely. After the meal, place your napkin on the table to the left side of your plate. Dab your lips when needed, and no ear to ear swiping or blowing your nose. If you drop your napkin on the floor, pick it up if you easily can. If it is out of reach, ask your server for another.

____

____

____

____

____

____

____

____

____

Do you think the alien will have an easier time learning how to use a napkin after reading the Napkin Rules or your steps?

____

The Three Little Pigs

Book reviews are printed in newspapers, magazines, or online. Sometimes they are read out loud on the radio. The reviewers provide the titles and authors of the books, as well as summaries of the stories. Then they explain why the book is worth reading or not.

Activity: Write a review of the book *The Three Little Pigs*. Think of a title for your review and include your byline (your name). Summarize the story, and then explain whether you think it is worth reading or not. Who might enjoy this story? Are there any parts that are especially enjoyable or terrible? Is there a lesson to be learned?

Title:

Byline:

The Wolf's Voice

Activity: Write a book review for *The Three Little Pigs*, only you are not writing as yourself. You are writing as a wolf! Use the word *I* when you write, but remember, you are a wolf!

Before you start, think about how a wolf might feel about this story. Would it like the way it ends? Would it like the way the wolf is portrayed? Would a wolf think that a pig that builds a house with straw is lazy?

Include a title and a byline (your wolf name) for your review. Summarize the story from a wolf's perspective. Then explain how you as a wolf feel about this story. Is it fun to read? Are there any lessons?

Title:

Byline:

Mammoth Cave

Mammoth Cave is in Kentucky. Over 390 miles of cave passages have been mapped there. Inside the cave, the temperature is about 54°F. It is so dark that people cannot see their hands in front of their faces. Tours of the cave have been offered since 1816. Some tours are simple walking tours that are short, while others are long.

One tour is very strenuous. People climb, crawl, and walk through parts of the cave that no other tour goes to. People need to walk in crouched positions and do lengthy crawls in spaces only nine inches high! They have to twist in and out of crawlway openings and cross jagged and rough rocks while on their hands and knees. The tour is over five miles long and lasts over six hours.

Activity: Write a paragraph in which you describe the kind of tour you would like to go on at Mammoth Cave. What is the perfect length and time for you, and how strenuous would it be? Explain why you would like this kind of tour and why the other tours would not be as enjoyable.

Night Vision

Imagine that you are on a tour of Mammoth Cave in Kentucky. Inside the cave, people cannot see without flashlights because it is extremely dark inside. However, when you walk inside, you realize that you don't need a flashlight. You can see in the dark! Do you tell people about your secret talent?

Activity: Write a story about what you do and see in the cave. Describe some adventures you have!

The Glass

If you had a drinking glass with water measuring up to the halfway mark, would you consider the glass half empty or half full? An optimist always sees the bright side. An optimist would say the glass is half full. A pessimist views things in a darker light. A pessimist expects the worst to happen and would see the glass as half empty.

Activity: Write two paragraphs. Both paragraphs should describe the same thing but from different points of view. One should be written with an optimistic voice, while the other should be written with a pessimistic voice.

You can choose your own paragraph topic, or you can write about one of the following:

- when you tried doing something new.
- a time when you got lost.
- what your dream job is.
- a trip you took to a zoo or park.

Read the paragraphs out loud to your classmates. Could they tell which paragraph was written with an optimistic voice?

The Spider

THINK ABOUT IT!

A huge spider escapes. It is somewhere in the classroom. Do you and your classmates eagerly look for it, wanting to examine it? Do you run and hide because you are frightened?

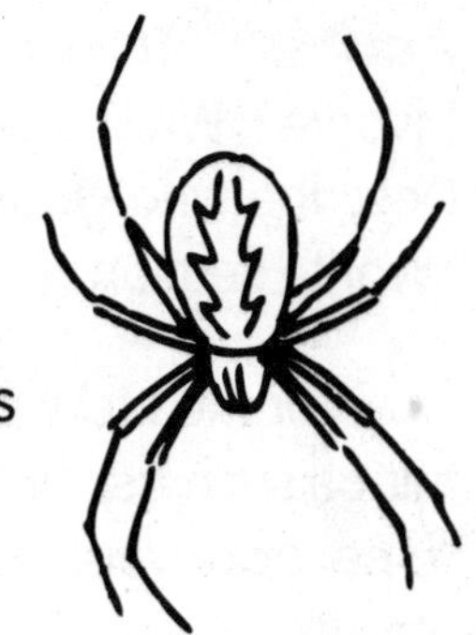

Activity: Write two paragraphs in which you describe what might happen and how people feel. In the first paragraph, show fear. Use words that make people feel nervous and afraid while explaining where and how the spider is found.

In the second paragraph, show amusement by using words that make people laugh. If you want, people at the end can find out that the spider is fake or harmless. You could even have someone accidentally step on it.

Read the paragraphs out loud to your classmates. Could they tell which paragraph showed fear?

Mystery Season

Activity: Think of the four seasons—summer, fall, winter, and spring. Which season is your favorite? Write a paragraph about your favorite season, using words that show how special it is. Describe what your surroundings look like and what activities you can do. Explain why it is your favorite season.

Now for the tricky part! Write your paragraph without saying the name of the season! Instead, say things such as, "My favorite time of year…" or "I think the world is at its best when…" When you are done, have your classmates read your paragraph. Could they guess which season you were writing about?

Why Seasons Change

There are many myths about the seasons. One myth is from ancient Greece. In the myth, Persephone was the daughter of the harvest goddess Demeter. Hades, the god of the underworld, fell in love with Persephone and took her to his underworld. Persephone's mom searched for her everywhere. Zeus, the king of the gods, told Demeter where she was. Then Zeus said Persephone could return to her mom for a portion of each year.

Why do we have seasons according to the ancient Greeks? When Persephone lives with Hades, Demeter is unhappy, and all the plants die. When Persephone returns, Demeter is happy, and all the plants grow again.

Activity: Now it is your turn. Make up a myth about why we have seasons. Your myth can be about an animal. It can be modern, or it can take place long ago. Use your imagination!

The Egg

Voice

You or a character you create finds an egg. After the egg is taken home, it hatches! How big was the egg, and what did it look like? How long did it take to hatch, and what came out of it?

Activity: Your hatchling or chick can be real or imaginary. Describe the egg and where and how it was found. Tell what happens when the egg hatches. Are people scared or excited? How fast does the hatchling or chick grow? Make your story interesting!

Organization

Big, Bigger, Biggest

THINK ABOUT IT!

When writers compare the size, length, or weight of a group of similar objects, they organize their writing in a particular order. They mostly talk about the objects in order from smallest to largest or largest to smallest. This makes the writing easier to follow.

Activity: Using the information about lizards below, write about different lizard sizes—either smallest to largest or largest to smallest. Add at least one detail about each lizard, but include the details immediately before or after you mention size. This will prevent your reader from getting confused.

Jaragua lizard: $\frac{3}{4}$ of an inch; can stretch out on a quarter

Gila monster: 2 feet; poisonous; eats eggs; in burrows 95% of the time

Common basilisk lizard: 2.5 feet; can run on water on hind legs because it has big feet with flaps of skin along the toes

Glass lizard: 4 feet; no legs; tail drops off and breaks into moving pieces

Marine iguana: 5.6 feet; can dive 30 feet underwater for 20 minutes; eats algae

Komodo dragon: 10 feet; world's largest lizard; serrated teeth can be 1 inch long!

The Pet

Organization

Activity: Write a story in which you or a person you imagine begs for a lizard pet. This person's parents say no at first. Then the parents say yes, but only if it's a very small lizard. Write about how this person feels after getting a pet lizard. Keep your story organized by describing what happens first, next, and so on.

Months

The months of the year listed in order are January, February, March, April, May, June, July, August, September, October, November, and December. You've probably had this memorized for years!

Activity: Write two paragraphs about the months in order. The first paragraph should be for the first six months. The second paragraph should be about the last six months. For each month, tell what month number it is and a detail about the month. The detail can be about you, such as a birthday or something you did, or a history or weather fact.

Example: *The month that follows February is March. March, the third month, is special to me because that's the month we visit my grandmother for her birthday.*

Hot December

DID YOU KNOW?

Seasons can occur at different times around the world. December is a winter month in the Northern Hemisphere and a summer month in the Southern Hemisphere.

Activity: Write a dialogue between two people. One person should be from the USA or Canada. The other person is from Australia. The two are confused about what each other says about the months. For example, Sherry (from Australia) says:

Sherry: *December is the best month for swimming in the ocean.*

Tamara: *Do you wear a wet suit to stay warm?*

Sherry: *Why would I need a wet suit when it is so hot?*

Air Conditioner Ears

The first sentence in a reading passage can affect whether the reader will want to keep reading or not. Which introductory sentence below grabs the reader's attention?

a. There is an animal with ears that are like air conditioners.

b. Elephants have big ears.

Activity: Copy the more interesting starting sentence from above and then finish the paragraph, using the facts in the left side of the box below to help you. Write a second paragraph about an elephant's trunk, using the facts in the right side of the box. Can you think of a fun sentence that will grab the reader's attention?

Elephant Ear Facts	Elephant Trunk Facts
African elephants' ears can measure up to 6.5 feet by 5 feet	both upper lip and nose
ears are thin with many blood vessels	more than 40,000 muscles (way more than you have in your entire body!)
elephant flaps wet ears on hot days to cool off	can push down a tree
cools blood as much as 10 degrees	can pick up a straw
cool blood cools elephant	sucks up water to drink, then empties into mouth
	uses trunk as snorkel when swimming

The Wish

Activity: Write a story in which someone makes a wish to be strong enough to push down a tree. The wish is granted, but not as expected! The person's nose is transformed into an elephant trunk that can be used to knock down trees! Tell how the person feels. Then write about how the new "nose" helps save people—perhaps when it was used as a snorkel or because of its ability to lift heavy objects. Don't forget to include a title!

Title: **Byline:**

The Bridge-Walking Elephant

It is important to order events in stories. If you don't, the story doesn't make sense. Order the lines below so that they make sense.

___7___ After Jumbo's walk, people trusted the bridge's strength.

______ The Brooklyn Bridge was built in 1883.

___3___ Jumbo was sold to Barnum & Bailey Circus in 1882.

______ Jumbo walked across the new bridge!

______ Jumbo the elephant was born in Africa in 1861.

___5___ People were afraid the bridge wasn't strong or safe.

___8___ *Jumbo*, meaning "really big," became a new word.

______ Jumbo was named in 1865 by zookeepers; the name most likely came from Swahili *jambo* (hello) or *jumbe* (chief).

Activity: Using the information above, write a complete story about Jumbo. Title your story "The Making of a New Word." Make sure the actions in your story are in the correct order. Add or change words to the lines above so that the story flows smoothly.

The Fruit

A story has an ending or a conclusion. Some stories have conclusions that make one think beyond what happened. Think about short stories or books you have read in which the author has started you wondering about what might have happened next. Have you read stories in which the events at the end were surprising or shocking?

Activity: Write a story with an ending that will make readers think. In your story, have two characters fighting over a mouthwatering piece of fruit. Describe the characters, the fruit, and the argument. Then, at the end, have the characters discover that the fruit is not real! It can be plastic, glass, or foam. For your final line, tell what lesson the characters learned. Don't forget to include a title!

Make sure that when you write, you arrange the events in order. You do not want the characters to know that the fruit is fake until the very end. If the reader knows before, the ending will not be a surprise.

The Holiday

Activity: Many cultures celebrate holidays in very different ways. Think of a holiday and describe the day, as well as the way in which you celebrate it. Before you write, plan ahead. Divide your description into two parts. The first paragraph should be about the holiday in general. What is its name, and what is it for? What is its history? The second paragraph should be about how you celebrate the holiday. How do you get ready, and what special things do you eat or wear?

Holiday	How I Celebrate

Something Is Wrong

Activity: Create a story in which you describe someone's morning. Explain how the person gets dressed and ready for school. Write about how they go to school. Tell how the person suddenly realizes that something is wrong because his or her surroundings seem different. Very few people are out, and the streets are quiet. Then the person realizes that it is a holiday! You can choose the holiday and how and when the person finds out. Make your reader wonder what is wrong, too. Don't tell that it is a holiday until the very end!

Greenland Letter

Activity: You are writing a letter to a friend. The friend thinks the country of Greenland and your country are alike. In your letter, tell your friend how the two countries differ.

Your letter should have two paragraphs. The first paragraph should describe Greenland. The second paragraph should describe your country. When you write, stay organized by talking about facts in the same order. For example, if the first fact you wrote about Greenland was where it is located and if it is an island, then the first fact you should share about your country is where it is located and if it is an island. If necessary, continue your letter on the back of this page.

Plan ahead by completing the information for your country in the chart below.

Greenland	(your country) ______________________
world's largest island that is not a continent	
less than 60,000 people	
capital is Nuuk	
exports shrimp and fish	
polar bears, musk ox, reindeer	
arctic climate	
81% ice-capped	

Dear ______________________________________,

My country is called ____________________, and there are many differences between it and Greenland. ____

____

____

____

____

____

____

Letter from Greenland

Activity: Imagine you have gone to Greenland. Write a letter to a friend back home. In your first paragraph, tell how you took a class for two days to earn your driver's license. The license is not for driving a car but for driving a dog sled with up to eight dogs! Describe a wild adventure you had while "driving" in your second paragraph. Make up any wild adventure that you want!

Light Around the Clock

Organization

What are you usually doing at midnight? Most likely, you are sleeping. If you were in northern Greenland, you might not be sleeping because it is the land of the Midnight Sun. It is light around the clock—all day and all night! From May 25 to July 25, the sun never sets. People can roller skate with the sun on their faces at two in the morning!

Activity: Complete the two event logs. One should be for where you live now, and the other should be for northern Greenland. Describe your activities.

May 25	Your Country	Greenland
8:00 a.m.		
12:00 p.m.		
4:00 p.m.		
9:00 p.m.		
12:00 a.m.		
3:00 a.m.		

Super Cat

Some say that cats are lazy because they sleep so much during the day. Have you ever wondered what they do at night?

Activity: Imagine that your pet cat is a Super Cat. You think it is lazy, but at night it becomes a superhero and has wonderful adventures. Fill in the event log for your cat. Include many details about what it does. Use your imagination!

8:00 a.m.	
10:00 a.m.	
12:00 p.m.	
2:00 p.m.	
4:00 p.m.	
6:00 p.m.	
8:00 p.m.	
10:00 p.m.	
12:00 a.m.	
2:00 a.m.	
4:00 a.m.	
6:00 a.m.	

Hurricane Eye

Activity: News reports tell *who, what, where, when, why,* and sometimes *how* things happened. Use the facts below to write a news report that is exciting to read. Make your sentences flow together. When you are done, write a headline that catches the reader's attention.

Who: Col. Joseph Duckworth, commander Instrument Flying School, and Lt. Ralph O'Hair

What: First to fly through eye of hurricane **Where:** Bryan, Texas

Why: Other British pilots thought the AT-6 plane wasn't sturdy! Duckworth wanted to show it was.

How: Breaking into the eye was an accident! **When:** July 27, 1943

Trip Details: Copilot Lt. O'Hair said the flight was like "being tossed about like a stick in a dog's mouth." In the eye, it was calm. They flew in circles inside the eye. The shape of the center was like a leaning cone. In the cone, they could see the sun and land. They flew into dark, overcast skies and rain to go home.

____

By: ______________________

First

Activity: Think of an adventure that you or someone else experienced for the first time. Perhaps you went to Mars or were swallowed by an octopus and lived to tell the tale. Use your imagination! Then write a news report about this first-time adventure. Include a headline and your byline. Before writing your story, plan ahead by filling in the blanks in the first box.

Who: ______________________________

What: ______________________________

Where: ______________________________

When: ______________________________

Why: ______________________________

How: ______________________________

Trip Details: ______________________________

____

By: ______________________________

Grocery Store

Transition words are words such as the following: *for example, when, soon, after, first, before, finally, next, now, then, immediately, suddenly.* Using these words helps to connect your sentences so they flow together.

Activity: Write a paragraph in which you are the narrator, telling about your trip to the grocery store. Describe what you buy, where you find it, how you transport (carry) it, and how you check out. You should purchase at least three items each of breakfast, lunch, and dinner foods. Be sure to include transition words in your writing.

Plan ahead! Grocery stores group foods. For example, dairy foods are all together, as are fruits and vegetables. If you are getting two different kinds of dairy foods, you want to get them at the same time. Also, think about when you want to put an item like ice cream in your cart.

	Breakfast	Lunch	Dinner
1.			
2.			
3.			

Jungle Walk

Using transition words will help your writing flow. Transition words are words such as the following: *for example, when, soon, after, first, before, finally, next, now, then, immediately, suddenly.*

Activity: Imagine that you are walking through a jungle. Describe what you see and what happens to you. Before you write, think about the location of your jungle, as well as the animals and plants that live in it. Use transition words to help you create a story that is realistic, scary, or humorous.

SCUBA

THINK ABOUT IT!

Using transition words will help your writing flow. Transition words are words such as the following: *for example, when, soon, after, first, before, finally, next, now, then, immediately, suddenly.*

Activity: A person asks you, "What kind of diving is scuba diving?" Write a paragraph in which you explain what scuba diving is. Your first sentence should inform the reader what you are writing about. Then provide examples of scuba diving and explain how the word *scuba* came about. Finally, share something about yourself. Have you ever been scuba diving, or would you like to? Be sure to include transition words in your writing.

Scuba Word Fact Box

SCUBA was first an acronym.*

S = self **C** = contained **U** = underwater **B** = breathing **A** = apparatus**

*An acronym is a word formed from the first letter(s) of words in a name or phrase.

**An apparatus is the tools or equipment used to do a certain job.

Man or Fish?

Organization

An alien comes to visit. The alien, coming from Venus, is unfamiliar with large quantities of water. You take the alien to the aquarium. You are standing in front of a massive tank when a scuba diver enters the water to feed the fish. The alien sees the scuba diver and gets very excited saying, "Look at that large fish!"

Activity: Write a paragraph in which you explain to the alien why the scuba diver is not a fish, even though he or she is breathing underwater. In your answer, provide examples of how fish differ from people. Be sure to include transition words, such as *before*, *finally*, and *now*, in your writing.

Autobiography

DID YOU KNOW?

A *biography* is a story of one's life written by another person. An *autobiography* is the story of one's own life written by oneself.

Activity: Write about your own life. Stay organized when you write! Don't jump from past to present and back to past. Try to stay on a timeline. What happened first, and what followed?

Your response should include at least two events in your life. These events may be about moving, starting school, learning how to do something, or gaining or losing a family member or pet. These events should happen after you discuss your birth. Describe what you look like and what you like to do. Write about your family, too.

500 Years Ago

IMAGINE THAT!

Imagine that you are the same age as you are right now, but it is 500 years ago. You live in the same place. What do you think your life would be like? Would your city exist? How would you get food and survive?

Activity: Write about your life. Do you have encounters with wild animals? Do you go to school? You can create any kind of adventure, but the details must fit the time period. For example, your story should not have any phones or cars in it!

Magellan's Trip

Activity: Ferdinand Magellan is known for leading the first trip around the world. Write a paragraph, first telling who Magellan was and what he was known for. Then describe his trip. Use transition words such as *first, second, next, after, before,* and *finally* to make your sentences flow. For your final sentences, explain why you think (or don't think) the trip was a success.

Ferdinand Magellan — Portuguese Explorer (1480–1521)

- 5 ships, 251 men
- September 20, 1519 — sailed across Atlantic from Spain to South America
- March 1520 — wintered in Argentina
- November 21, 1520 — first to sail from Atlantic to Pacific when he went through the Strait of Magellan
- March 16, 1521 — landed in the Philippines
- April 27, 1521 — killed in the Philippines
- September 6, 1522 — one ship, with 18 survivors, came back to Spain

Sailing Trip

Activity: Imagine that you are on a sailboat, and you are going to sail to all the continents! Select a starting location and then write about your other stops (in order) before you sail back to your starting place. Report how long you stay at each stop. To save costs, you want to keep your sailing time to a minimum and not have to backtrack or retrace your steps. Think about where you will go before you write! Then record your route. Using transition words will help your writing flow.

When you are done, compare your route to other students' routes. Did more people go around the world west to east or east to west?

Riddles

DID YOU KNOW?

Riddles need to be told in the correct order. The question must come before the answer. Some riddles are funny. If someone doesn't understand a riddle, it needs to be explained.

Activity: Read the riddles below. Imagine that your friend does not understand the answers to them. Choose one riddle and write a paragraph in which you tell the riddle and explain the answer. Then give your opinion—is the riddle funny or not? Do you know a funnier riddle?

Q: What do you get when you cross a rooster and a duck? **A:** A bird that gets up at the quack of dawn!

Q: What kind of horses go out after dark? **A:** Nightmares!

Q: Two silk worms were in a race. What was the result? **A:** A tie!

Q: Two flies are on the porch. Which one is the actor? **A:** The one on the screen!

Conventions

Space Walk

Remember, capital letters are used for . . .

- the start of sentences. (**L**et's go swimming!)
- proper names. (**S**an **J**ose, **C**alifornia)
- titles of books, songs, movies, and articles (short words like *a* or *the* are not capitalized unless they are the first word), such as ***L**ittle **H**ouse on the **P**rairie.*

Activity: Read the paragraph, and add proofreading marks when necessary. You will need to add the following:

- 10 marks for uppercase letters Example: texas
- 7 marks for lowercase letters Example: Fish

something Happened for the first time on february 7, 1984. bruce mcCandless left his Spacecraft. bruce was an Astronaut on the space Shuttle *challenger*. Other people had left for Space Walks, but bruce's walk was different. bruce was not tethered to the *Challenger*. He was not tied to anything. if something went wrong, he would float away. there would be no getting Back.

Activity: Now show what you know! Write a short paragraph with at least four sentences. In your paragraph, explain what you would like to do if you were an astronaut. Where would you like to go, and how long would you want to be gone? Would you be willing to go outside without a tether?

Include five uppercase and five lowercase letter errors in your writing. Write the incorrect words correctly on the back of this page. Show your test paragraph to your classmates. Could they spot the errors?

Counting Chickens

Remember, capital letters are used for . . .

- the start of sentences. (**E**at and be merry!)
- proper names. (**N**ashville, **T**ennessee)
- titles of books, songs, movies, and articles (little words like *a* or *the* are not capitalized unless they are the first word), such as ***T**he **F**ox and the **G**rapes.*

Activity: Read the paragraph, and add proofreading marks, when necessary. You will need to add the following:

- 10 marks for uppercase letters Example: washington
- 5 marks for lowercase letters Example: Rain

patty lived in corn city, iowa. It was july 9, 1832. Patty was about to Carry a pail of milk to the Market when she told her mother, "i'll sell this milk and buy some eggs. The eggs will hatch, and I'll raise some Chickens. Then i'll have eggs to sell, and i'll be rich!" patty twirled around in Excitement at the thought of being rich. That's when all of Patty's milk spilled. patty's mother said, "Don't count your chickens before They have hatched."

Activity: Now show what you know! Write a short paragraph with at least four sentences. In your paragraph, write about someone who went to sell butter on a hot day. Have this person learn not to "count his or her chickens before they have hatched!"

Include five uppercase and five lowercase letter errors in your writing. Write the incorrect words correctly on the back of this page. Show your test paragraph to your classmates. Could they spot the errors?

Tick Volunteers

Activity: Read the paragraph, and add proofreading marks when necessary. You will need to add the following:

- 4 periods (**.**)
- 1 question mark (**?**)
- 1 exclamation mark (**!**)

Ticks are parasites that carry diseases A study was done by scientists to find the best insect repellent. The scientists asked for volunteers to put insect repellent on their legs Then each person stepped into a tub with 100 ticks in it The ticks were lab-raised, so they were disease free Would you ever volunteer for this kind of study If you said "yes," then you are very brave

Activity: Write an advertisement asking for volunteers for the insect repellent study. Try to make people want to volunteer. Check that you have used ending punctuation marks correctly when you are done.

World's Largest Cupcake

Activity: Read the paragraph, and add proofreading marks when necessary. You will need to add the following:

- 1 period (**.**)
- 1 question mark (**?**)
- 2 exclamation marks (**!**)

A bakery in Minnesota made a cupcake that could be the world's largest cupcake It weighed 150.7 pounds The icing alone weighed 60 pounds Do you think a cupcake this large could still taste delicious

On April 30, 1988, a banana split was made that used 33,000 bananas, 2,500 gallons of ice cream, and 600 pounds of nuts. The dessert was 4.55 miles long!

Activity: Imagine that your school wants to make the longest banana split in the world. Write an advertisement asking for donations and volunteers. Verify that you have used the correct ending punctuation marks when you are done.

Deer Tale

Activity: Cross out the eight misspelled words in the letter below.

Deer Brady,

Boy, do I have a tail to tell you! The tail is a great story. It is about a dear without a tale. Oh deer friend, you will not stop laughing when I tell you how the dear got a new tale!

Do tail/tale and deer/dear sound the same? ___ **yes** ___ **no**

Do these word pairs mean the same thing? ___ **yes** ___ **no**

THINK ABOUT IT! **The word pairs above are homonyms. Homonyms sound the same, but they do not mean the same thing. When you write, you need to use the correct spelling. Otherwise, the reader may not know what you really mean.**

Activity: Write a short letter to a dear friend in which you tell a tale about a deer. Have you ever seen one? What do you know about them? Do they have tails like lizards that can break off or tails like monkeys that they can wrap around things? When you are done, check that your spelling matches the meaning!

The King and the Rain

Activity: Match the three words below with their correct meanings.

rain	**strap of leather on a horse's bit**
reign	**to rule as a king**
rein	**water droplets that fall from the sky**

Activity: Now imagine that you are a king or queen. Create a name for the country that you reign, and describe a day when it rains and rains. Tell how a horse has gotten loose and is scaring everyone. Explain how you catch the horse's reins and make it stop.

Include many details in your story. For example, what scared the horse? How big was it? Was it dangerous to catch the horse's reins? When you are done, reread your story and add a title. Check that your spelling matches the meaning!

Title:

The Chocolate Bar Accident

When you write, you need to check your spelling because the reader will take your writing more seriously if the words are spelled correctly. The reader will also know exactly what you mean. There is a list of the 100 most commonly misspelled words. What words are on the list? One word is *accidentally* because people forget to include two Ls!

Activity: Cross out the two misspelled words in the paragraph below.

Percy Spencer, an engineer, had a chocolate bar in his pocket. While he was standing next to a magnetron tube, the chocolate bar accidentaly melted. That accidentaly melted bar helped change the way we cook! It led to the microwave oven we use today! Before, scientists did not know that microwave energy could cook food. They were using microwaves to spot planes.

Activity: Now write about a time when you accidentally did something. You might have forgotten a name or an object, tripped, or went to the wrong room. Explain what you learned or what happened because of what you accidentally did. When you write, use the word *accidentally* at least two times. Make sure you spell it correctly!

The Amazing Pudding

Activity: Make up a funny or scary story in which you accidentally make amazing pudding. Decide what is amazing about the pudding. Is it magical? Does it never disappear? Does it make you strong or not need sleep? It is your choice!

Include many details in your story. Tell what happens with the pudding. Be sure to use the word *accidentally* in your story!

When you are done, review what you have written. Check your spelling and capitalization. Verify that you have the correct punctuation marks at the end of your sentences.

You're or Your

The words *you're* and *your* are often misspelled. The words *you're* and *your* do not mean the same thing. When you write, you want people to understand what you mean and take your writing seriously. You want to use the right word.

You're means "you are." (Example: You're late, so we missed the bus.)

Your means "it is yours" or "it belongs to you." (Example: Your hair is black.)

Activity: Cross out the misspelled words in the sentences. Then write the correct spelling.

You're name has five letters in it. ______________________________

Your going with me to the mall. ______________________________

Activity: Write what four people are to you. Then write something that they have. Use the words *you're* and *your* at least one time for each person. Write two to three sentences for each person as though you're writing directly to them.

Example: *Emily, you're my good friend. Your black-and-white dog is named Spot.*

1. ____

____

____

2. ____

____

____

3. ____

____

____

4. ____

____

____

Now go back and check your spelling. If you can say "you are," the word should be spelled *you're*.

The Note

Heidi Hippo received a note that said the following:

> *Dear daughter,*
>
> *We found an island in the middle of a lake that we need to buy. We will be safe there, and your welcome to visit any time. All we need is for you to send some of you're money.*
>
> *Love,*
>
> *You're mother*

Heidi Hippo took the note to Detective Dingo and said, "I know that this note did not come from my mother."

Detective Dingo asked, "How do you know?"

Activity: Tell Detective Dingo why Heidi Hippo knew the note did not come from her mother. Write what the note would have looked like if her mother had written it. (Hint: Heidi Hippo's mother was an English teacher.)

Seahorses

You can combine two short sentences into one long sentence by doing two things.

1. Put a comma (,) after the first sentence.
2. Add the words *and, or,* or *but* between the sentences.

Example:

The mother seahorse lays the eggs.

The father seahorse carries them in a special pouch until they hatch.

The mother seahorse lays the eggs, but the father seahorse carries them in a special pouch until they hatch.

Where is the comma? ______________________________

What word connects the two sentences? ______________________________

Activity: Combine these two sentences into one sentence using the word *and.*

A seahorse can move one eye at a time. Like a monkey, it can wrap its tail around a stationary object .

____

____

Activity: Write two short sentences about two different kinds of pets you could have. Then combine them into one sentence using the word *or.*

short: ______________________________

short: ______________________________

long: ______________________________

____

Activity: Now write two short sentences of your own. Then combine them into one long sentence using the word *and, or,* or *but.*

short: ______________________________

short: ______________________________

long: ______________________________

____

The Pet Horse

Activity: Write a story about a student who keeps insisting that he or she has a pet horse that lives in his or her bedroom. All the kids and adults tell the child it can't be. Then on show-and-tell day or when someone visits the child's house, they find out that the child does have a pet horse in the bedroom—a pet seahorse!

When you write, form at least two long sentences by combining two short sentences with the word *and, or,* or *but.*

When you are done, review what you have written and add a title. Check your spelling and your punctuation. Did you remember to put the comma before *and, or,* or *but* when you joined two complete sentences together?

Title:

Two Faces

How do we know what someone is saying in stories? We put their words in quotation marks (" "). We put commas (,) to separate their words from the rest of the sentence.

Activity: Look at the example below. Circle the commas and quotation marks.

Abraham Lincoln was in a debate. A debate is when each person has a different side to argue. A man insulted Lincoln during the debate. The man said, "You are two-faced."

Did the comma go before or after the quotation mark? ____________________

Did the period go before or after the quotation mark? ____________________

Activity: Now fix the sentences by adding the missing comma, question marks, and quotation marks.

What did Lincoln say He said If I had two faces, do you think I'd be wearing this one

Activity: Now it is your turn to write! Write a paragraph that includes at least one quotation. Use the following as a guide:

First lines: Say what Lincoln was doing and how he was insulted.

Middle: Tell what the man meant when he called Lincoln two-faced. Tell how Lincoln turned the insult into a joke.

End: Tell how you feel about what Lincoln did.

____

____

____

____

____

____

____

____

Cats and Dogs

Activity: Write a conversation between two cats, two dogs, or a cat and a dog. Have the animals debate as to what makes better pets—cats or dogs.

When you write, change the start of your quotations by using words such as *barked, meowed, purred, yelped, growled,* or *hissed,* instead of *said.*

Example: Kitty purred, "Of course cats are better than dogs!"

When you finish, review what you have written. Check your commas and quotation marks!

B or P

Do spelling and writing clearly matter? Oh, yes, they do! Look at the letters that make up the two words below. What is the only difference between the two words? ______________________________

beaches **peaches**

Activity: Write two short paragraphs. Begin your first paragraph by telling how spelling and penmanship can make a difference. Then add some facts and information about beaches. For example, you can tell about a beach trip you have taken or want to take.

Write about peaches in the second paragraph. End your paragraph by saying if you can eat a peach at the beach or eat a beach at the peach.

When you finish, review what you have written. Did you spell everything correctly?

What's that We're Eating?

Activity: Write a story about a misunderstanding with at least two paragraphs. In your first paragraph, describe your characters. Explain how one of the characters does not want to go with his or her friend because he or she thinks they are going to eat beaches.

In your second paragraph, have the person find out they are eating peaches. Add many details, and tell what each person is thinking. When does the person find out it is *peaches* not *beaches*?

When you are done, review what you have written, checking for neatness and spelling.

Thank-You Letter

What is wrong with the first lines of this thank-you letter?

I wants to thank you for the gift. My sister want to thank you, too.

When you write, you want your verb to agree with your subject.

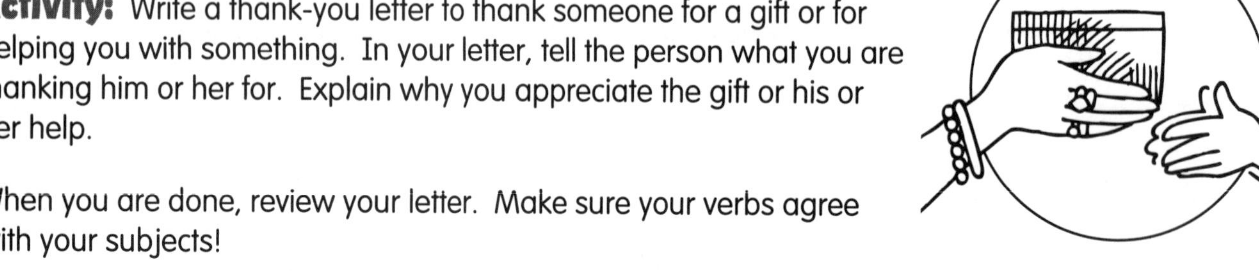

Activity: Write a thank-you letter to thank someone for a gift or for helping you with something. In your letter, tell the person what you are thanking him or her for. Explain why you appreciate the gift or his or her help.

When you are done, review your letter. Make sure your verbs agree with your subjects!

Dog Thank-You

Imagine that your silly Auntie DeeDee mailed your dog a gift of an old shoe and an old tennis ball. Before the box arrives, your aunt calls you. She says, "I can't wait to read the thank-you note your dog will send me. He's so clever!"

Activity: You know dogs can't write, but you want your aunt to be happy. Write a thank-you note to your aunt. Remember, you must write as if you are a pet dog. In your note, tell Auntie DeeDee what you are thanking her for, and then explain what you will do with the gifts and why you appreciate them. Add many details to your letter, and sign your note with a dog name.

When you are done, review what you have written. Make sure your verbs agree with your subjects.

Who Is Drinking What?

Activity: Underline the verb in each sentence. The verb tells what the person did to his or her drink.

Dezi sipped her drink. **Meg choked down her drink.**

Nessa drank her drink. **Steven tasted his drink.**

Activity: Tell which four people from the above sentences are most likely doing what. Then explain.

	Who	Why
taking medicine		
drinking something very hot		
with friends at lunchtime		
trying something new		

Each person had a drink, but the verb helps the reader picture the action in the story. Now it is your turn to write!

Activity: Think about all the dogs and cats you know. Choose one that you think seems really mean and another that seems really nice. In one box, write about how the mean animal makes you feel. In the other box, write about how the nice animal makes you feel. Write three or four sentences in each box. Use verbs that will help the reader understand how you are feeling. Then read your sentences out loud or show them to another student. Could they tell which box was about which animal?

Animal 1

____

____

____

____

Animal 2

____

____

____

____

Marvelous Meal

Activity: Write a short story. In your first paragraph, tell how you are trying to make a marvelous meal. Describe the ingredients, as well as how you want people to feel about eating the dish.

In your second paragraph, describe the dining experience. Will it just be you or other people, too? Tell how no one likes the meal. Use action words so the reader can imagine how horrible the dish tastes.

For your last paragraph, surprise your readers. Tell about someone coming and taking a bite. Report how you and everyone else were shocked to find that the person likes the dish.

When you are done, review what you have written. Check your spelling, punctuation, and grammar.

Break a Leg

What is an idiom? An idiom is a phrase that means something other than what the words seem to mean. Idioms may be hard to understand if you are a non-native English speaker or are learning a new language. For example, consider the phrase "a piece of cake." These words can mean part of a cake. When used as an idiom, they mean that something is very easy. These two meanings are not the same at all!

Activity: In which sentence is the phrase "a piece of cake" used as an idiom?

1. I ate a piece of cake at Ellie's birthday party.
2. Counting by 10s is a piece of cake.

Activity: Write a paragraph in which you explain the idiom "break a leg." In your paragraph, describe what an idiom is. Discuss what saying "break a leg" can mean and then tell what it means when used as an idiom. Include the information from the box below when you write. Why might an English learner need to know this?

Theater News

People in theater think it is bad luck to say "good luck" before going on stage. They say "break a leg" instead. For actors, "break a leg" means good luck!

Buying a Lemon

An idiom is a phrase that means something other than what the words seem to mean. The following are some examples of idioms:

- "buying a lemon" (buying something that doesn't work correctly)
- "drive someone up the wall" (annoying someone)
- "raining cats and dogs" (raining very hard)
- "cat got your tongue" (having trouble speaking)

Activity: Choose an idiom from above or another one you know. Write a story about a new student who is learning English, and include a scene in which an idiom is used. The new student gets very confused because he or she does not understand what the idiom means. You can write your scene in paragraph or dialogue form.

Proofreading Marks

Proofreading is when you read over what you have written to check for mistakes. How do proofreaders illustrate what is incorrect? They use certain marks, such as the following:

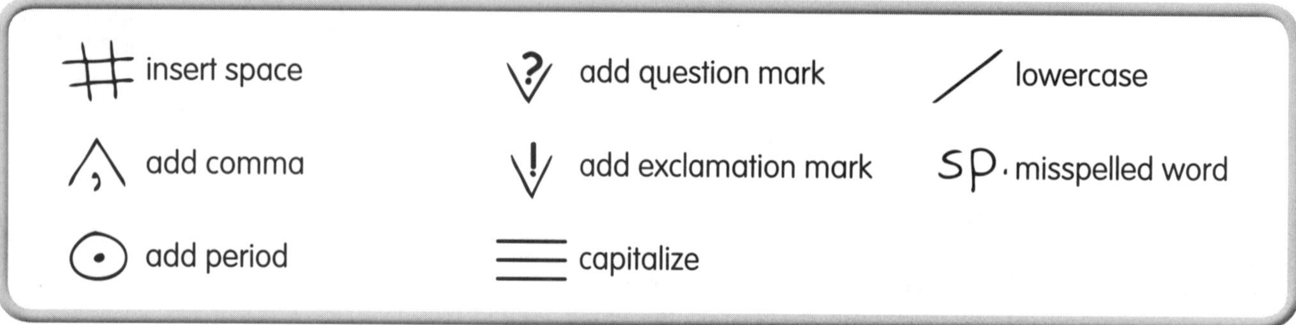

Activity: Proofread the passage below. Add the proofreading marks as needed to correct the mistakes. You will need the following:

- 1 question mark
- 1 misspelled word
- 2 uppercase letters
- 2 lowercase letters
- 1 period
- 1 insert space
- 1 add comma

an insect's skeleton is outside of its body. Whot is an insect's skeleton called It is called an exoskeleton. The exoskeleton Supports the muscles insidethe body. It protects the insect Like a coat of armor Insects will shed their exoskeletons in order to grow. the new exoskeleton is soft but then it hardens.

Activity: Now show what you know! Write some sentences about your skeleton. Tell where it is located, what it does, and if you can shed it. Include any bone facts that you know. Your sentences should contain some mistakes. Mark the mistakes with the correct proofreading marks.

____

____

____

____

Skeleton Collection

Activity: Read the following sentences. Add proofreading marks to correct the mistakes.

Did you no that crabs have exoskeletons Crabs will Molt all of their lives but they molt less often as they age.

Activity: Now write a story about a person who has a skeleton collection. You or others think the bones are from people when, actually, the bones are crab shells! Make your story scary at first, but then have a funny ending.

When you are done with your story, review it and add five mistakes. Include proofreading marks by the mistakes.

Titles

When you write, you want a title that is appropriate for your story. You also want to remember these rules:

- Always capitalize the first and last word of a title, even if they are short.
- Capitalize all important words (verbs, nouns, pronouns, most adverbs and adjectives).
- Do not capitalize most short words in the middle of the title (such as *and, for, a, the*).

Activity: Correct this title: a place for jenna ______________________

Tell why you capitalize *a* even though it is a small word. ______________________

Write two titles for each type of book following the guidelines above. You can make up your own titles or use titles from real books.

Mystery

1. ______________________
2. ______________________

Nonfiction

1. ______________________
2. ______________________

Fairy Tale

1. ______________________
2. ______________________

Instructional

1. ______________________
2. ______________________

Adventure

1. ______________________
2. ______________________

Writing Prompts

Prompt 1

You are in the circus. Would you like to be a clown, an animal trainer, a tightrope walker, or another circus act? Why? Name some good and bad aspects about living as a nomad. (Nomads do not live in one place. They move around.)

Prompt 2

I was shaking, but I took a deep breath to calm myself. Then I . . .

Prompt 3

What is the latest you have ever stayed up? Include many details. Tell when, where, with whom, and why. How long did you sleep when you finally fell asleep?

Prompt 4

Suddenly there was a loud crash. Then there was a loud roar. Then . . .

Prompt 5

"Be patient," Eric said to his little sister. "I only have three hands." . . .

Prompt 6

Write a story about a pet that saves a family or person. The pet can smell smoke, keep someone from going somewhere, or not allow someone to touch or eat something.

Prompt 7

What is the difference between a photograph, a painting, and a drawing? Give an example showing when each one would be better than the others.

Prompt 8

You wake up and your hands are invisible! Write a story about what you do and how you feel. It is up to you if your hands become visible or not by the end of the story.

Prompt 9

In 1736, Ben Franklin wrote, "Fish and visitors smell in three days." What do you think he meant? Do you agree (fully or partly)? Give an example or two that supports your answer.

Prompt 10

An octopus has no bones. It is entirely soft-bodied except for some cartilage in its head. (Your nose and ears are made of cartilage.) For this reason, an octopus can squeeze itself through a hole slightly larger than its eye. Imagine you have a secret power where you can squeeze through a hole the size of your eye. Create an adventure story in which you use your power.

Prompt 11

You are traveling to a different country. Name the country and the ten most important words you should learn before your visit. Explain your choices.

Prompt 12

My heart almost stopped when I opened the door and saw who was there. I . . .

Prompt 13

If you owned your dream business, what kind would it be? What kinds of things would you sell or do? Where would the business be located, and what would your hours be? Would you make your employees wear uniforms?

Prompt 14

You are walking to school when, suddenly, a small frog jumps on your shoe. You go to nudge it off, and the frog says, "Kiss me, and I will . . ."

Prompt 15

Would you rather parachute out of an airplane or ride in a hot air balloon? Explain why. Describe what you see as you look down.

Prompt 16

Imagine that it is 100 years from now, and you live on the moon. What might your day be like? Where do you eat and go to school? What do you do for fun?

Prompt 17

All of a sudden, it was like a lightbulb went on in your head! You had broken the code! "Oh boy," you whispered to yourself. "Now . . ."

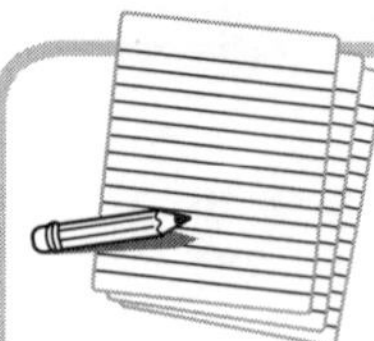

Prompt 18

Your friend, sister, or brother is very sad. How could you make him or her feel better?

Prompt 19

You felt a tap on your shoulder. You turned around, and someone who looked like a boy said, "What planet is this?"

Prompt 20

You are in the park and you see something strange on a tree. You walk up to the tree and see a small door. The sign on the door says, "Do not knock." Your friend says, "I wonder why not?" and then knocks.

Prompt 21

You wake up and go downstairs. An old man comes in. It is your younger brother! He is now much older than you. You slept for 50 years! You stayed the same, but everyone else aged. Write a story about what you do after you wake up.

Prompt 22

You can go back in time for one day. What time would you go back to? Would you just watch, or would you try to change something? Explain your answers.

Prompt 23

The bottle on the table says, "Drink me." You carefully unscrew the cap and . . .

Prompt 24

You can read people's thoughts. Give three reasons or examples of why this is a fantastic talent. Then give three reasons or examples of why this is a terrible talent.

Prompt 25

Carla could no longer feel her hands or her feet. She was so cold, but she knew that if she stopped she would freeze to death.

Prompt 26

Should scooters or skates be allowed in the mall? Explain why or why not. Should there be exceptions for some people?

Prompt 27

Ben looked in horror (or astonishment) at the snake. He had never seen one this large before. It was moving toward him!

Prompt 28

If you could meet one famous person, who would you like to meet and why? What activity would you like to do with him or her? What is one question you would definitely ask?

Prompt 29

Would the singing ever stop? It was driving Sam crazy! . . .

Prompt 30

You are being given a free ticket. What event would you like a free ticket to? It can be to anything—a game, a movie, an amusement park, a concert, or even a plane or boat ticket. Explain your choice.

Prompt 31

Rachel was reading her book at the library. Suddenly she began to tingle. Then she felt herself being pulled into the story!

Prompt 32

Your job is to give one million dollars away. You can give it in one lump sum, or you can divide it up. The money must go to people who need help or to organizations that help others, animals, or the environment. Who will you give the money to? Explain your choice.

Prompt 33

The orangutan at the zoo pointed with his hand. You look down and see the key to his cage!

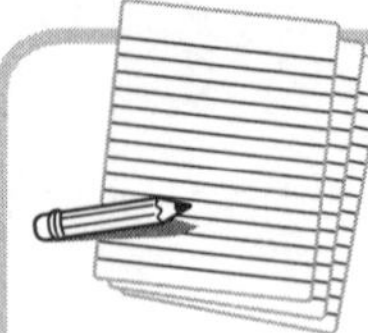

Prompt 34

Describe a place where you feel safe. Tell why. Include many details so that your place cannot be mistaken for another place.

Prompt 35

"I wish my hair would grow faster," Lee said as she (or he) walked past the store with the strange statue in the window. Suddenly, . . .

Prompt 36

How is your state different from Alaska and/or Hawaii? How is it the same?